Love Without Lust

Peter N Muya

Published by Peter N Muya, 2024.

Love Without Lust

Peter N Muya

Published by Peter N Muya.

DEDICATION

I dedicate this book to the youths and also to my grandsons, granddaughters, Gathoni, Njoroge, Maina, Alex and Trina. May the lord rescue the youth before they are lured or enticed by their own lust for when lust has been conceived gives birth to sin and sin when it is fully grown brings forth death. (James 14:15)

Lust is not love
Bishop PETER N. MUYA

Foreword

DO YOU WANT TO DIFFERENTIATE between the lustful love of the world and God's redemption love? Read this book by my friend and co-worker, Bishop Peter N. Muya. I know him personally and his wonderful ministry of Gospel Messengers Church in Nakuru City, Kenya. Every year the young people are lured by their bodies to engage into illicit sex, which results into unwanted pregnancies and abortions.

Valentine's Day is the evil day when they meet to celebrate love in all forms, including engaging in illicit sex. You will meet them in the streets buying flowers for their girlfriends and after that paying for having sex. If you are looking for a heartwarming and romantic read that will introduce you to God's unconditional and redemptive love, I highly recommend Love Without Lust.

This beautiful book explores the idea that God's redemptive love can be rekindled and reignited even after having being born again and changed. The story will tell you how the author was changed by the Word of God and how he left his former girlfriend. It was a shock for his girlfriend, Nelly, to receive a letter. "I will never be associated with you for God's sake," the letter read in part. Do you think it was easy to break this deep love relationship that had lasted for years? With engaging characters, vivid descriptions and touching story, this book will leave you smiling, laughing and falling in love with God, the creator of all things in heaven and on earth.

This is what the author is calling "Love Without Lust." This agape love is unconditional and redemptive. I like this captivating book because it portrays God's redemptive love in all walks of life. Whether you are looking for an escape from hell or from evil behaviors, or you are saved, but you want to be rekindled, reignited, this book, *Love Without Lust,* is a must read. Get your copy today and fall in love with God all over again.

The author, Bishop Kamau Kabatha, and Dr. Kwake, have started a publishing company to help Christian authors who want their books to reach the world before it's too late. I would recommend you to try TRIELITE PUBLISHERS in Nakuru City. They have a range of promotional opportunities to help your book reach a wider audience. This includes your targeted market. If you are looking to publish your book with reputable guys, please try them. I am sure they will give you the satisfaction you desire. I shall be looking forward to reading other titles by my friend, author and publisher, Bishop Peter Njoroge Muya.

Enjoy reading this and other titles.

Bishop Kamesh Soul winners International Ministry

Acknowledgement

I WANT TO THANK MR. Kamau my English teacher in my school days. I have clear memories of his writing lessons. He helped me develop some Writing skills which have made me write meticulous books. Also, I would like to thank Alfred E. Stillwell of Troon, Aryshire, Scotland, who taught me how to write Christian articles many years ago. Thank you Pattin Roberts for designing the cover.

A note of thanks to Mrs. Ester Wambui from the New Hope Center, Nakuru who typed the manuscript, not forgetting her father the late John Njau Chege for his Prayers and moral support. Many thanks to the pastors and members of the Gospel messengers church Nairobi, Nakuru, Bomet, Kisii, Gilgil, Tanzania, Rwanda, Congo and Uganda. Lastly let me thank my editor Wambugu Revival Springs Magazine, Peter Hinga, and proofreader Christine Dye, Goldleaf Editing Services USA.

THIS IS A TRUE STORY of how Gods sacrificial love arrested me. This book, Love without Lust, gives the youth tips on how to live a holy life by chilling out from sexual lusts after obeying Gods word and waiting until the wedding day. What is lust? It is a very strong desire to have or get something. Many people in this hurting world are having a strong lust for power, fame and wealth. Women are having a strong lust for beauty while the youth have a very strong lust for illicit sex. That's why we have unwanted pregnancies and abortions.

The bible warns "But each person is tempted when he is lured and enticed by his own lust. Then lust when it has conceived gives birth to sin, and sin when it is fully grown brings forth death" James 1 -14 – 15.

God's sacrificial love is different from the lustful love of the world because its redemptive without strings attached, "But God shows his love for us in that, while we were still sinners, Christ died for us "Romans 5-8

This is how God's sacrificial love arrested me "Love is strong as death" (songs of Solomon 8-6) A glance of faith at the Calvary marks on Christ's body, will silence your every excuse, your sins of refusing a free pardon at the cost of the savior's blood will sink you into external death in Hell forever.

That's why Paul told Timothy "Flee sexual lusts, pursue righteous, faith, love and peace" (2nd Tim 2-22). He also told him "To abstain, from fornication" (2nd Thess 4-3) the book is about total abstinence from illicit sex and waiting until the wedding day.

Introduction

IT'S TRUE THAT MY LIFE was miserable as a drug addict, but suddenly, without notice, God's redemptive love arrested me. My life changed completely when this unconditional love burst in my heart like a timed bomb. That's when I surrendered my life to Jesus Christ and confessed my sins. I wiped the sweat in my face with the covers of my bed and I discovered that it's a fearful thing to fall in the hands of the living God (Hebrews 10:31).

I obtained a new life that was very different from that of the world. It was not a self-planned experience or emotional, yet it affected me all over, mentally, spiritually and physically.

Over the years I have been tremendously brought up spiritually by the members of Kiambogo Full Gospel Church in the village. They cared for me, encouraged and taught me how to behave as a Christian. I will never forget how they happily shared their little resources with me when they noticed that I was in dire need.

To my former girlfriend, Nelly, and my closest friend, Kim, I was looked upon as a stricken buffalo that had left the herd. I knew I was set free from the lustful love of the world, but I did not know how I could tell them how it happened.

What I wanted them to know is that I was a changed person, delivered out from this crooked and lustful generation into the chosen generation. Out of the sidelines into the witnessing platform. No more illicit sex, no more drugs, no more discos and no more drinking the illicit brew in the ghettos.

In 1979 Rev. Mbugua invited me to a soul winner's seminar conducted by the famous Evangelist T.L. Osborn from America. The seminar was held at Menengai High School, Nakuru City. The topic was soul winning. When the servant of God laid his hands on us at the end of the seminar, I was slain in the Holy Spirit for minutes. When I gained consciousness, I discovered that I had received something that was more than silver or gold—I received a double portion anointing.

In the village together with my pastor, we started preaching the gospel and winning souls for Christ as never before.

The purpose of writing this book is to reach the youth and persuade them to escape from the lustful love of the world and seek God's everlasting love. We are changing them from their evil behaviors and introducing them into the kingdom of God. Thank God they are changing their behaviors, and they are joining the church.

I want you to evaluate your evil behavior and call Jesus Christ to deliver you from sins. When I received Jesus Christ as my personal savior, the church recognized that I was a good soul winner and they appointed me as an evangelist. Later I became a pastor, and I married Mary Gathoni in a church wedding. We were blessed with three kids who are now adults.

God has helped me to open churches in Kenya, Tanzania and Uganda. The wonderful love of God has made me to be what I was called to be—a soul winner. This agape love of God is what I call "Love Without Lust." Read this book and you will discover this important theme that made me to be what I'm today. God bless you.

BISHOP PETER N. MUYA.

CHAPTER ONE

WHY WAS I BORN

WHY WAS I BORN? I ASKED myself. There appeared nothing special about me, a drug addict who hated and cursed his own life. Seemingly I was born one of these indolent, irresponsible, poor creatures whose life in this world must turn out to be either pitiful, or tragic. I was born and brought up in a small village in Lanet, some fifteen kilometers from Nakuru town. My parents were extremely poor. They usually sat beside our mud hut, wondering what would guarantee our survival. Now I know that it is only the great mercy of our God that kept them from committing suicide. With their rugged passion, they brought me up in a life punctuated by the joys and sorrows of a hard existence. The bad conditions of life adversely affected my mind and I nurtured a paramount interest in political rather than social issues.

During my early days of boyhood, my parents planned to enroll me in an upcountry school. At my desk in class, I had feelings and intuitions like those of a little rural boy. During my time there I worked very hard with a goal to attain a good life in future in order to support my poverty-stricken family. After several years in school, I transferred to another school. This was mainly through the efforts of my mother. As a result, life at home became a little easier as the family members agreed with me that she had indeed made the right decision. In the event I also improved in class work performance.

As I left home, I promised to take caution. My parents released me to go to town in pursuit of more education. In the new school I had the reputation of a very naughty boy. Although fellow students saw me as a social misfit, I became my class favorite pupil. He would write in my report form that my efforts at teacher's school were remarkable. He said good things about me that I was likely to perform well in the end. During the weekends, my new friends took me round the town and showed me many exciting things and places. I was strangely surprised by such a life, which I knew little or nothing about.

Although I had left home with a desire to study, I became involved in the affairs of the world. I became a frequent visitor to public places like cinema halls, disco halls, social halls and nightclubs. With the 'friends' I made in town I was able to roam about and get acquainted with the surroundings. With time, I became a figure to reckon with, at times brushing shoulders with local politicians in bars. Just like a naïve upcountry boy. I determined to identify with town peer groups, though I would learn to be civilized. But the end results saw me utterly confused. My pals didn't help me much as they used to reach back in feats of laughter after witnessing my poor imitation gimmicks.

On Sundays, I would go to the disco-halls. Getting in through the open door, the disco lights would change my appearance. The ladies inside there would think that I was a director with an international firm in Kenya. My face was likewise known in various movie halls. I was regarded as a great merchant in town. Only a few knew that I was a school dropout who had messed his school fees.

During that time, I did my revision and examinations in the public halls, rather than in the school. One day, I assessed both the quantity and the quality of my life, remembering my mother's warning before I left home. I began to shed tears. I remembered the great love of my poor family, especially the act of sharing their daily bread with me, as my school fees. When I considered the life of my family, I was challenged to go on with my studies. Before leaving school, I applied myself with so much diligence to my studies. Luckily enough, I passed my examination, but very narrowly. Then I was out of school, struggling hard to make ends meet. I began wishing that my parents were millionaires. If they had not used the whole lot of their money on me, probably they would have done business to get rich. "Oh God!" I cried. But who was to blame?

I cursed my parents bitterly for bringing me into this world. I cursed my life. I displayed my bitterness openly by writing on the back of my old jackets, "WHY WAS I BORN? I was wandering from place to place like a helpless vessel in the ocean. I was a poor creature with no dignity in life. I accumulated a lot of bitterness in my desperate condition to which no solution was forthcoming. Just like a beetle lying on its back, I was completely helpless. I did not know the works of God, "As you do not know how the Spirit comes to the bones in the womb of a woman with child, so you do not know the work of God who makes everything" (Eccl. 11:5)

A life without meaning! There was no sense for me living in this world any longer. The thought of committing suicide flashed in my mind. Mine was a life of misfortunes, failures and a lot of burdens. All my friends and relatives deserted me. I waxed deeper in sin, suffering and much shame. Therefore, I hated life, because the work that is wrought under the sun is grievous unto me for all is vanity and vexation of spirit, (Ecc. 2:17).

Slowly by slowly, I became an alcoholic, a drug addict, a sexual-pervert and an excessive smoker. These evil and crooked ways were my masters. But time came when I began searching for unknown something, which could give relief to my tortured soul. I tried everything the world could offer. But, there seemed no hope of finding a successful cure for my condition. I began to choose friends according to their ability and desire for earthly pleasure. I liked those who drunk anything bitter. "Woe unto them that rise up early in the morning that they may follow drink; that continue until night, till wine aflame them," (Isa.5: 11). But my dear family planned to protect me by taking me out of the town to Kiambogo farm and placing me in custodial care as a mental case.

The fear of being committed to a mental institution became an obsession to me and I completely yielded to their plans because I believed they would protect me. I was given a plot where I was expected to clear bushes and use it for farming business. With the help of a panga, a jembe and an axe, I became a charcoal burner who hated and cursed his life.

I was finally confined and put out of contact with decent society. All my life and education was fully focused on rural development. After several years in the farm, I became a devoted rural farmer in my home area. I was gradually impressed by the farming business, which brought great happiness in my life. Just try to imagine planting only a few seeds and waiting for a great harvest within a short time. I thank my dear family for their thought to rescue me. Let me say that farming is a good business but it puts very many youths off. I was happy with farming business especially when I started earning some money and with it, I learnt to be satisfied.

My parents had tried to rescue me from the sinful life of town by taking me to Kiambogo farm in Elementaita. But in the terrible boredom of the up country life, I was thinking about Nelly. I could never imagine that, one day her name will sound so terrible in my ears. To me Nelly was a beautiful queen. She was always happy and friendly. I thought I would marry her and settle down to discover what love is all about. But I only defiled and left her to bear the shame alone.

Nelly was a wonderful town girl. She was young and smart, calm by nature. She was my girlfriend. We used to walk together in town boldly. In the up country, life was very boring, but memories of her kept me going, though I had failed her terribly.

But we were both lost in sin. I knew that I had messed Nelly's life; for I was jobless and not ready to meet her needs as a husband. I did not own anything. As I thought about my life and how I had messed Nelly's life, I felt as guilty as a murderer. I was stricken with grief and despair was all written on my face. This realization made me want to end my life.

Several chaps of my age had done it before. I remembered one incident, which involved my friend. It was foolish for one to commit suicide, I thought. It happened to me as my father had told me once, "Young man, there will come a time when all your friends will deny you and the world will use you, and then fail you. You will wish you had listened to me. My son, I beg you to reform, and then realize the helpless predicament you are in, before I die."

Was the old man right? I asked myself. All my intimate friends detest me, those I love turned against me. I am nothing but skin and bones" (Job 19:19, 20 NIV). I was a bad boy. I was corrupt, cruel, dishonest, and a slave to evil powers. I was trapped through enticements of Satan and the passions of the body. I was overcome by drug-addiction and alcohol. I was a disco-dancer with many traces of permanent physical damage. I was engulfed in anguish and despair. "If only my anguish could be weighed and all my misery placed on the scale! It would surely outweigh the sand of the seas..." (Job 6:2-3 NIV).

A feeling of desperation and helplessness passed through me as I remembered my hopeless situation. I was a teenager of 23 years and I had nowhere or turn to for help.

One day my elder brother, David Muya, who at one time was worse off than me, came to me in the garden. He was holding in his hand a Bible and when he gave it to me, my heart skipped a beat. The first words I read made me want to discover more of the Bible "FEAR NOT, ONLY BELIEVE" (Mark 5:36). He told me to read the Bible and further persuaded me to change my sinful ways of life and receive Jesus Christ as my savior. He assured me that God loves me then left me to read the Bible on my own.

As I perused the pages, past memories of my livelihood shone vividly in my mind. I remembered my religious background and realized I was lost. A great conviction took hold of my stubborn heart. This made me consider my ways and ask for forgiveness as I decided to return to my God. To be frank, I was fearful the conviction would not last. Many times I had made resolutions that faded with time. Little did I know I was to come out of uncertainty and doubts unto a faith which is absolute truth without a shadow of doubt.

My soul was now focused on the love of God. I had to remember how, with other youths, we used to flock all corners of Nakuru town in search of dangerous drinks. "Woe unto them that are mighty to drink wine and men of strength to mingle strong drink" (Isa. 5:22). I remembered my former life where I was brought up in a very humble way of life. Through the efforts of my mother I attained good education. My family had sacrificed much through hard times for my upkeep. Surely it could be very hard for us children to survive if it were not for my mother who cared for our welfare and mostly our school fees. She made money by hard and even risky means of brewing the illicit liquor "chang'aa" at night to escape the police dragnet.

This outlawed business was the lifeline of our family's income. My brothers and sisters were willing participants in this bad illegal business and even other worse money making ventures in the name of survival. I was profoundly disturbed by the bad traditional ways and hardships in which I had been brought up. I could not help them to come out of the bad habits for I did not know any scriptural quote of the Bible. For me to stop such a great business that made us survive was to make the life of my family uncertain. I started to cry as I thought deeply about my poor family.

At home a friend gave me a book of Billy Graham that explained to me on how to be born again. The title was "WORLD AFLAME." As I read page by page the word of God became real to me that Jesus was knocking at the door of my heart. "Behold I stand at the door, and knock (Rev. 3:19).

In the morning, I rose earlier than usual, and set myself to consider what Jesus could do to my sinful life. "Oh Jesus." I cried but there was no answer. I could now feel the terrible weight of my sins. "I will complain in the bitterness of my soul." (Job 7:11 NIV).

Sitting on my bed, I thought, "Will I be able to define the story of Jesus briefly to my girlfriend Nelly?" My mind was helplessly puzzled by this dilemma, for I was resolving to forsake Nelly once and for all. "No!" I said with consciousness. I was not willing to lose the pleasures of this world yet.

All these evil thoughts crossed my mind, but soon they were buried down by the story of Jesus which was in the bottom of my soul. After all, how shall I attain this supernatural power which will help me to overcome the evil love for Nelly, which is disturbing me? I wondered.

What will she say once she knows of my newly found faith in Jesus, I thought with a humble heart. "What I feared has come upon me, what I dreaded has happened to me. I have no peace, and quietness, I have no rest, but turmoil" (Job 3:25, 26 NIV).

I was all alone to make the final decision. I knew I was to be opposed by all men of my age group but I was ready to live a new life without sin. "Have pity on me, my friends, have pity for the hand of God has struck me. Why do you pursue me as God does?" (Job 19:22 NIV).

I had not heard any message on the new life in Jesus before, but now, as I read the Bible through, I learnt that to die unforgiving and unchanged was to perish in hell. I was assured that I had despised the laws of God. Never in life had this awful truth from the Bible been so plain to me. I looked again at the captivating words of God, "Fear not, only believe." I felt Jesus standing by the door of my heart, waiting for me to welcome Him.

After much reflection from the word, I promised God that as soon as my season of youthful amusements was past, I would devote myself to eternal pursuits but the words kept ringing in mind. I felt forsaken by the world and God standing by me. Although at first I had no love of God in my heart, no repentance, nor did I wish to forsake sin. I felt nothing but solemn gloom and despair. I was now in the mighty hands of my creator from whom I expected mercy. "Hide thy face from my sins, and blot out all mine iniquities." (Psa. 51:9).

Reading through the Bible I became more and more acquainted with the Lord Jesus Christ and believed that He would forgive my sins. I was fully convinced of this, for I had no other hope for my wretched condition. I knew from the gospel that it is a must for me to repent my sins and receive JESUS CHRIST as my personal savior. Although I learnt this from the book I planned to ignore the call of Christ due to my preference for pleasures of sin.

This was my greatest burden, which I had to lay in faith before my Lord. What a terrifying experience this is? I wondered.

I was badly off financially. In my small hut, I had no stool or table, only a small lamp beside the bed-rail. Because I was a bachelor, I did not worry much, although I had no money and didn't expect any. Due to such hard times I often felt worthless.

I lay prostrate on my bed with my hands pressed over my ears to shut out the outside world of sin and concentrate on Jesus instead. I had a heart full of longings and compassion for this unseen lover of the world Jesus! Yes, He is real and now I believed that He paid everything for my sins, even the sins that I committed in childhood. People would not understand it, I thought, but Jesus loves me. Yes, I wanted this Jesus, but my attention to evil thoughts also disturbed and tortured me greatly.

There was a great battle in my mind. Somewhere within me there was a voice which disputed this love of Jesus. Another voice told me that time had come for a decision, and Nelly had nothing to do with it. Definitely I had to lose Nelly and receive this universal lover—Jesus—or otherwise perish in hell eternally.

At night I went to bed as usual, and for this reason I could not sleep. I, therefore, decided quickly to have Christ as my savior. I thought of saying a little prayer and certainly, without wasting time I went down on my knees and I prayed. Soon I felt the touch of God in my soul, the battle began. I did not know exactly what was happening, but I felt something very real and frightening that took place. I tried to move out of bed but I could not.

There was such a powerful free Spirit, which was holding me tight. I felt very sorry for my sins, for I knew that I had made a mess of myself. I felt power in my soul and I cried to God in faith for help in a loud voice, "Have mercy upon me, Oh God, according to thy loving kindness, according unto the multitude of they tender mercies blot out my transgression. Wash me thoroughly from mine iniquity and cleanse me from my sins. For I acknowledge my transgressions; and my sin is ever before me. Against thee, thee only, have I sinned and done this evil in thy sight; that thou mightiest be justified when thou speaketh, and clear when thou judges." (Psalms 51:1-4).

I thanked God for saving me. I found myself lying in bed helplessly, bathed in sweat. I had asked for the power of JESUS CHRIST. He came and caught me by right arm, picked me up, then wrapped His nailed hands around me. I felt fresh after the blood of Christ cleansed me everywhere in my senses and conscience. All this happened in the Spirit and in my soul. God's power crushed every sin and the evil in my heart was removed and now I felt the Son of God, virgin born, in my soul. He died for me on the cross. I saw Him standing looking at me with eyes full of compassion and great grace. He gazed at me, and then He said to me personally, "Fear not, I am Jesus."

God's love burst in my heart like a timed bomb. I mourned bitterly for my life, and rubbed my forehead with the bed covers to wipe the sweat. "It's a fearful thing to fall into the hands of the living God." (Heb.10:31). Jesus came in my heart, I heard His voice in my heart saying, "Fear not, I'm Jesus" truly His name is love. My heart was throbbing within me. I breathed heavily and I was trembling in the presence of Holy God.

If I had listened to the voice of the evil spirits, I could have killed myself and spent my life in hell for eternity. "Have I any pleasure at all that the wicked should die? Says the Lord God and that He should return from his ways, and live." (Eze. 18:23). I will not let anybody tell me that there is no salvation, for Jesus is life and strength. "Neither is there salvation in any other. For there is no other name under heaven given among men, whereby we must be saved." (Act 4:12).

I was somewhat relieved; I lifted up my head, not yet conscious of all that had happened. I did not know what to say, since there were some powers holding me tightly, although now I could not see anything or anybody nor could I hear anything. I sat on my bed, my face wet with tears and my mouth was full of saliva. I felt very weak as if some of my muscles had been ripped from my body. I could now consider the past; the untidy, unplanned past and it made me feel pity and shame before my God. I could not cry anymore; I wiped my face like a child who recognizes the power of his loving father.

I thought again of my former life and discovered that I was a hard creature, grown in sin and evil. I was like a victor from a battlefield who finds an escape from a prolonged bombardment, it was with much pleasure that I realized that Jesus loves me and was real to me. My heart was filled with joy and peace. I turned slowly beside my wooden bed, I struck a match and lit my small lamp and found that there was nobody in sight but there was someone in my heart. He was real.

I could sense that I was no longer alone. There was power and unseen somebody in my heart, this I knew was certainly Jesus. Instantly, after this experience, I was back in my body sitting in bed with a tremendous awareness that I had just been saved from death unto life through the blood of Jesus Christ. I was made alive when I was delivered from sexual lusts. I was also freed from the prince of this world.

All the spirits of demonic oppression were gone and I was free from sin, lusts of the flesh and the desires of the heart. "By nature

I was a child of wrath like the rest of mankind. And you hath he quickened, who were dead in trespasses and sins; where in time past you walked according to the course of this world, according to the prince of the power of the air, the spirit that now worketh in the children of disobedience.

Among whom also we all had our conversation in times past in the lust of our flesh, fulfilling the desires of the flesh and of the mind; and were by nature the children of wrath, even as others. But God, who is rich in mercy, for His great love where with He loved us, even when we were dead in sins, hath quickened us together with Christ (by grace ye are saved); and hath raised us up together, and made us together in heavenly places in Christ Jesus." (Eph. 2:1-6).

CHAPTER TWO

DELIVERED FROM SEXUAL LUSTS.

WHEN I WAS BORN OF my mother, she nurtured me as a baby and brought me up, but now in Kiambogo, twenty something years afterwards, I was born again of the spirit. I was delivered from sexual lusts. I received a new life that is different from the natural life. I obtained a life that is everlasting and of peace. It was not a self-planned experience; it was not emotional, yet it affected me all over: mentally, spiritually and physically. I praised the LORD that night with joy, which is unexplainable. It was until later that I learnt many wonderful lessons on the subject of this new birth. I knew that something thrilling had happened in my life.

The next thing I knew was that I was awake and delivered from sexual lusts. Immediately felt that my confused mind was healed. I also remembered that Jesus had told me to trust in Him. He promised me that He would lead me until I see His face again. Truly Jesus is real. "His name is Love." I proved it.

Early the next morning, I woke up and went to tell my brother David about my new experience. I began by telling him everything that had happened since I saw Jesus. I told him the whole story and he was amazed, and anxiously listening because he 'd passed through the same experience one year ago. He took his Bible and quoted to me this scripture: "Therefore, if any man be in Christ, he is a new creature: Old things are passed away, behold, all things became new." (1 Cor. 5:17).

Before I experienced this new birth I was not happy, I was always striving to attain something worthy for my future. But now everything in my life was laid before my Lord Jesus who cares for me more e than I do. Since then success seemed the most important thing in my life.

I became a successful soul-winner in my village and this brought me real joy, peace of mind and a new assurance for my future. My life was completely covered eternally in Jesus Christ "For ye are dead, and your life is hid with Christ in God." (Col. 3:3). I found myself being changed from sexual lusts by supernatural power into a Christ loving, Bible reading and praying Christian. This is a miracle! No works of mine was required. But the moment I believed so it happened – Hallelujah! "For by grace are ye saved through faith, and that not of yourselves, it is the gift of God." (Eph. 2:8).

To my old pals, they were not satisfied with my changed life. They considered me a stricken deer or buffalo that left the herd. I was a different creature before them. I was in a different world where I freely talked about God in every opportunity and tried to win souls for Christ in every spare moment. I often sang hymns in church and at home instead of the popular pop music, which I used to sing before.

This proved that I was completely a different person in my old friends' eyes. I knew how the change took place, but surely I could not make them understand until they experienced it themselves. As for me, my inner eyes had been widely opened to the realities of the spiritual world. I realized that the Bible was really the voice of God that, when obeyed, can cause miracles to happen.

I saw that the Bible was full of wonderful promises for me. It also revealed to me tenderness and nearness of God in Christ which satisfied my heart's longing and showed me that the infinite God is the creator of the world who took our nature upon Him that we might be one in His great love.

I believe in the Bible because it reveals a religion adapted to all classes and races in the world. The Bible states clearly that all people are the same worldwide. I believe that it is an intellectual suicide knowing all this and not believing it. Perhaps one of my strongest reasons for believing the Bible is that it revealed to me a spiritual diagnosis for my condition. It showed me clearly what I was by nature—one who was lost in sin and alienated from the life that is in God.

I found it to be consistent and wonderful revelation of the character of God, who removed me from my natural imaginations. As faith continued to reveal God to me, I could go without question whenever He led me. I always put His assertions and commands above every seeming probability in life and I entertained cherished convictions. I can trust Him through whatever would happen in the course of believing Him.

I'm always prepared to stand alone when declaring Him to be the truth, the way and life worldwide. "The LORD is my light and my salvation; whom shall I fear? The Lord is the strength of my life; of whom shall I be afraid?" (Psa. 27:1). Had He not told me personally? "Fear not, I'm JESUS." I shall never forget this phenomenon in myself.

Reading the Bible and listening to God's voice, I found answers to my problems, which had long troubled me. I therefore, learnt to pray and claim these promises in faith and I saw other miracles happen before my eyes. My faith is built on nothing else but the word. Here is my prayer. "Create in me a clean heart, O God; and renew a right spirit within me. Cast me not away from thy presence; and take not thy Holy Spirit from me." (Psa. 51:10-11). I thank God for the wonderful way He intervened in my life and made me to know that He has called me to the ministry. I also thank Him for revealing to that my vision is – "Reaching Africa for Jesus."

CHAPTER THREE

I WAS BAPTIZED IN THE HOLY SPIRIT

THE PROMISE IS – "BUT ye shall receive power, after that the Holy Spirit is come upon you: and ye shall be witnessed unto me both in Jerusalem and in all Judea, and in Samaria, and unto the uttermost part of the earth." (Acts 1:8).

And so it is my privilege to tell you how God pursued me with His love and saved me from sin and filled me with His Holy Spirit and so I became a power-packed gospel messenger. I thank God for His intervention in our family which made me and my brother to be close friends. God is good. He has remained real in my life since.

To me God is not merely a belief in my heart but power in my life. He intervened in my life and I knew that He would direct me throughout. Yes! In Christ not only was I saved from sin, but in Him I found answers for my life. For the first time after knowing this truth, I attended Full Gospel Church on Sunday at Kiambogo. I publicly confessed Jesus as my personal savior before members of the living church, which is also the body of Christ.

They joyfully welcomed my testimony with cheers of hallelujah! I therefore committed myself into that spiritual assembly of believers. During the services I began to learn experimentally one course after another. Truly the Lord is real to all those who seek to live by faith and not by the law. Even as our physical bodies cannot do without food & water, nourished Christian requires spiritual food and water. Jesus said – "It is written, man shall not live by bread alone, but by every word that proceedeth out of the mouth of God." (Matt. 4:4). I live by the word.

During the service, I found everything to satisfy my spiritual thirst and I joyfully perceived all in the LORD. After the sermon we prayed together and I heard everybody praising in the spirit and speaking in other strange languages. How could I keep quiet with such things happening? I encouraged my melting spirit.

After the service, as I was going home alone, I came by an older brother, a man whose godly conversation quickened my faith and he invited me to his home. I felt the presence of God in his house and his wife's testimony was in the spirit's quickening power. I also felt a warm glow of God's love flowing in me and I joyfully committed myself into that Christian home assured that I had been guided by God into a real spiritual home.

After taking tea together, they asked me whether I was baptized in the Holy Spirit. I said, "No," although I knew nothing about the Spirit. They willingly took their Bible and taught me from the scriptures. They read to me (Acts 1:8). "You shall receive power after the Holy Ghost is come upon you and ye shall be my witness unto me."

They later asked me to thirst for the spirit as they fully assured me that God is always willing to fulfill His promises to anyone who believes. I was dumbfounded and I did not say anything. After tea I left for home, but the words were still ringing in my mind.

At home in my small hut, I was challenged and decided to experience this endearment with power, for now I believed that I was not an acceptable worshipper or even an effective witness without this power from heaven. All night I prayed and read the word to myself. I dedicated my life to God fully. I sighed and groaned from morning till night expecting the baptism but unfortunately nothing happened.

I tried to confess every sin I knew, but Satan suggested many reasons why I could not obtain this blessing from God. I had no power to pull back these doubts, which were the great enemies of my faith. All I could do was to cling to God hopefully and expect Him to fill me with his Spirit. Gradually a feeling of despair crept over my soul threatening to swamp me.

As I waited before God in silence, a thought came in my heart, God speaks so quietly: "How did you receive Jesus as your personal savior?" Then a voice said: "The Holy Spirit is received in the same way." Surely we learn through mistakes, all I was to do was to confess with my mouth that the Lord has just filled me with His Spirit Amen! I was to receive and then begin to praise God.

Now I realized that God was speaking to me personally in His word while I was straining to read Luke chapter eleven, verse thirteen. "How much more shall your heavenly father give the Holy Spirit to them that ask Him." But I questioned myself: "God, why have I asked several times and not received?" And a voice said: "Read Mark chapter eleven, verse twenty four."

I read through: "Therefore I say unto you what things so ever ye desire when ye pray believe that ye receive them and ye shall have them." The word "believe ye receive" clung to my heart and I understood that although I had prayed all night I had not believed. I was now commanded by God's word to believe that he gave me the Holy Spirit when I first prayed. This was contrary to all those traditional ideas I had formed in my mind concerning the baptism. Suddenly I understood that faith was not a matter of waiting until I felt some heaven sent experience of the incoming power but it was rather a matter of accepting the gift of the baptism of the Holy Ghost and power by faith.

The Promise

The promise stood: "Ye shall receive the gift of the filling of the Holy Spirit." And as I believed, so it happened. Praise the Lord! I was filled by the power of the Holy Spirit in the deepest part of my being and then I understood that any gift of God cannot be earned by long prayers or brought by any works, but it is a free gift by faith only. I had not obtained the blessing because I tried to work for it. No. I had expected heavenly-sent sensations to assure me that God had answered my prayers.

This is not faith at all; everything God gives to His sons is on the basis of a gift received by faith. If anyone does not have faith, it is impossible for him to receive anything from God. The Bible says, "Without faith it is impossible to please Him." (Heb. 11:6). Through experience my eyes were suddenly opened from the blindness of my unbelief. In faith I offered my life completely to God to dispose of it as it pleases Him. In my heart I could trust in Him fully through whatever would happen, knowing that God is my refuge at every storm.

How wonderfully God leads His sons by His Spirit, when their inner eyes are completely fixed on Him; and yet some carnal Christians are in the churches because their relatives lead them therein. It would be interesting if every professing Christian would get down in faith before God and ask for the baptism of the Holy Spirit. The spirit will flow in you after believing and God will give you a definite guidance through the spirit as to where you will have fellowship. I'm sure that many carnal churches would quickly be emptied for the liberating power of the Holy Spirit would quickly break the chain of sectarianism. I do rejoice in the spirit, although I do not forget to watch carefully those carnal Christians who secretly oppose me.

Yes! I received the baptism of the Holy Spirit in my life as I believed the word, but I had no clear proof of whether the Holy Spirit was working in me. I cannot forget to remember that my former friends could not stand my bold speech about God and His wonderful salvation, so they always avoided me and went away cursing. By this reaction I knew I was a different creature before them.

I Spoke In Tongues

One Wednesday evening I went to have my usual prayers with other brethren. I knelt down and prayed with tears of joy flowing down my cheek. I had a wonderful experience of the endowment with power.

I was overwhelmed by waves of divine power and I heard myself praying aloud, speaking in tongues. I prostrated myself helplessly before the Lord and brethren, unable to get up till the power abated. I embraced the brethren. I was not an emotional man and I was not expecting such an experience of endowment with power.

God rewards faith when He chooses and in spite of the protest of the carnal brethren who did not accept my experience as being genuine or scriptural, I witnessed to them without adding my own views about that experience. I took my Bible and read (Act 1:8) to them aloud: "Ye shall receive power, after the Holy Ghost is come upon you and ye shall be witnesses unto me."

One brother among the carnal brethren accepted my testimony as scriptural for he received the spirit and we became joined by God's love and we worked together. But on the side of my opposers they had some difficulties in accepting my experience because their ministry was the mere letter of the word. They were ministers of the letter. "The letter killeth but the spirit giveth life." (2 Cor. 3:6).

From that moment I became used to praying. I would pray many times in a day, I even learnt to ask other blessings from God in faith. Once I simply asked for the power to fill me. I believed God gave that to me and I began to thank Him for blessings received even before seeing the results. This I knew was the way of faith. Sometimes after believing I felt nothing at that time, but a little later I was filled with power of the Spirit in my life in the deepest part of my being.

Praise the Lord for His faithfulness to all those who live by His power. I also received extra joy which is unspeakable and full of glory. I even enjoyed speaking in tongues daily, for now I became an effective witness of Christ and I had a quickened revelation of the scriptures which made the word of God alive in me always. I also used to praise the Lord in my village as my mouth shouted a deep, "Amen."

The Opposers

The power of the spirit that I received helped me to overcome trials in my life, and this made me not to care about the carnal brethren who openly opposed me because their testimony was very different from mine. We have these carnal Christians in every spiritual gathering. So please brother or sister, take care. "But by their fruits you shall know them." Gradually, however, I was hanging on praising which made a living fire that was burning fast in my soul.

I began to witness in my home village and the church. And the joy of the Lord began to fill my heart while it grew till it became unspeakable joy. I always felt like bursting with praises as my witness began to rise with greater power. I saw that Jesus was alive in me and was standing on my side. So I had nothing to worry about. I could not remove my eyes from the risen Christ nor stop the Hallelujah's from rising to my lips.

Some Christians would ask me, "Brother Muya, do you speak in tongues?" and I would say, "Yes! This is the first glorious sign of the spirit's infilling." Today, some false teachers are teaching that there is no need of speaking in tongues. Do you accept this life from hell? These false teachers are in every nation telling Christians that the baptism happened once at Pentecost. But I would request you to read your Bible well and you will find that others were filled in later days after Pentecost. Read for yourself – (Act 8:14-17, 9:17, 10:40, 11:16 19:16).

"I thank my God; I speak in tongues more than you all" (1 Cor. 14:18). Let me give you my living testimony, I'm very much interested in speaking in tongues more than any other Christian in the world. My faith is focused on all the promises in the word of God. I'm always determined to be satisfied with nothing less than the promises. I live by faith in the word. When I speak in tongues I'm building myself spiritually. (1 Cor. 14:1-5).

Showers Of Blessing

At the initial reception of the spirit I was filled with power, but later I learnt that there was no need to keep on asking, all I was to do was to ask once and receive. Jesus taught, "If any man thirst let him come unto me and drink." (Jn. 7:37) I could have received the Spirit of power at that time, of my salvation but only I had not known the truth about it.

As a young Christian I had very few spirit filled believers to teach me, not to mention those who rebuked me. How I thanked brother Kimani who was a good teacher to me. To be filled with the Spirit is to keep on drinking every day, deeper and yet deeper all the natures of God. And this was to purity, adorn and expand me to every God's given capability to man. Where there is no spirit, there is no revelation, no witness, no conviction and there is no repentance. That is why many churches in the world are dead, because they do not bring men to a saving grace.

When God revealed this power in my soul, I started to grow, just like a young plant and God was watering me with showers of blessings from heaven. I could burst in praises for I was now in a new life of generosity in giving, new patience in sorrow, new touches of faith, new dreams and visions. All this brought me to the real existence of the fullness of the spirit of God in my life.

This is the way that brought my life into the open heaven of heavens and it can bring the same blessing to you Christians if only you believe. Hallelujah! It is obvious that all God's promises to every believer are appropriated by faith. Thus, we as Christians ought to ground our faith in the living word of God. So now remove doubts and fear and receive the promises of God in His word.

As a genuine Christian you must be baptized in the Holy Spirit just like the early Christians. This is a promise to every true believer of Jesus Christ. What about you? Where do you ground your faith? This is how I received the Holy Spirit by faith and that's why I am cheerfully privileged to instruct and lead many others in Africa and even in the other regions beyond into this wonderful blessings. I always pray to "Be filled with the spirit, (Rom. 5:18). "and I will make them and the places round about my hill a blessing; and I will cause the showers to come down in his season; there shall be showers of blessing." (Eze. 34:26).

Rivers Of Living Water

There is no genuine spirit-born child of God who does not long to have rivers of blessings flowing in his life. The great passion of

God to bless men, even at the cost of the Calvary sacrifice of His own son, burns in the heart of every spirit filled Christian. It is true that God's spirit can seem to be weak through frustration and disappointment, but it is always ready to split into a flame given a fresh breath of hope. Out of death comes life in nature, and it is the same in the spiritual realm.

God often allows His earnest child to come to a place of utter despair, like Abraham, Jacob, Joseph, Moses, etc., before He quickens this faith and uses him greatly. If you feel that you are at such an experience in your Christian life, do not be discouraged, because the moment of quickening your faith has come. "Behold I have refined thee, but with silver, I have chosen thee in the furnace of affliction." (Isaiah 48:10).

Before Jesus began His ministry, He first went into the wilderness to be tested by the devil. So every minister of the gospel must be willing to pay the cost for the anointing. It's very costly. Receive the Spirit now, and the river of living water will flow in you. Yes! That promise can be fulfilled in you when you are completely dead in the flesh. God, who received you in your sins and embraced you in eternal love, still longs to give you heaven's best blessings.

You know well that this is true, why then don't you lay your sins and past failures on Jesus Christ now and believe that His blood cleanses you and His spirit will fill you afresh. It is a matter of willingness and faith. Are you willing? Will you believe now? Jesus says to you now: "He that believeth in me as the scriptures hath said out of his belly shall flow rivers of living water." (John 7:38). Jesus is the fountain of the living water, why don't you believe Him and live by His wonderful power.

These promises are not made for special men and women of great ability, or ministers, missionaries, evangelists, great preachers;

it is offered to anyone who believes. As a Christian I expect you to know well about faith. The moment you believed that the work of Jesus at the cross was for you personally, that He has removed your sins away there, that moment became true in your life and Jesus entered into your heart and you were saved instantly.

Pardon is a free gift, which you can take from God's hand by faith. It is the same faith that Jesus wants you to have so that you may receive the rivers of blessings in your life. If you thirst for the Holy Spirit to fill you in your heart, Jesus says, "Come unto me and drink." If you thirst for the blessing to pour out on others then you simply, "drink in faith from His never failing springs." Jesus will be in you, for you, just what you believe Him to be! You will have all what you want now. Receive now and begin to praise God.

Endowment With Power

Ask the person who has received the spirit or the endowment with power how he received it, he will tell you that it is a gift which is received by faith. Nothing is demanded in payment. Are you willing? But do not make the mistake of thinking that God is going to make you another Billy Graham or Oral Roberts, T.L. Osborn, Reinhard Bonnke, Morris Cerullo, Schambach or duplicate of any other servant of His. No, each one of us is unique to God and He wants to use every one of us as His Heavenly vessels as He sees fit, for He needs all kinds of workers in His kingdom. Will you trust Him completely to fit you somewhere?

No matter what or where He chooses for your service, the rivers will flow as He promises. If you keep on with Him, keep on drinking from His fountain, which is always full of living water. You will never be thirsty in this dry world of today. Believe in Him fully and your little abilities God will multiply. You must give yourself to God fully and be willing to pay the price, so that God can release His anointing to you. The anointing is not free. You must pass through the fire of God before he makes you a power packed gospel messenger.

So don't be ashamed of your little abilities, trust Him all times and He will bring it to pass and the river of living waters will never cease to flow in your life. Cast all your sins and human failures in the empty grave of Christ and live in the fullness of His resurrected life. A vessel full of sweet water is set before you now, and I request you kindly to take it in faith and say. "Thank you Lord for baptizing me with your Holy Spirit, Amen!"

It is my prayers that God will fill you with the Holy Spirit and then send you out where He needs you most. God bless you indeed. Pray with us for a great revival in Africa. Our Motto is: "To preach the gospel to every creature."

Reading the Bible days and nights, I understood my part. I became an effective witness for Christ. That it was not merely the words I spoke, but the words of the Spirit and life. Jesus was speaking His inspiring words through my lips. I saw evidence of the word to sinners who were often becoming aware of eternal blessings in Jesus Christ.

One day, it occurred to me to see what the Bible said about itself. I took a good chance and worked out the word. I looked it again and again and found out that the Bible claimed from one end to another to be the authoritative word of God to man. I only planned to take this holy book as the source of my life; even now I do believe the Bible to be the inspired word of God, inspired in a sense utterly different from that merely human book. I would encourage you to receive the Holy Spirit, so that you can be a power-packed gospel messenger.

CHAPTER FOUR

LOVE WITHOUT LUST

THIS GREAT CHANGE OF life was surprising, not only to my family, but to all others who knew me as a crook. To all I was completely a new figure. I was in a new kingdom where I was set free from all sorts of false love like that of my former girlfriend.

Truly I was saved, but how could I convince Nelly Muthoni? Definitely she would at once protest against faith, but I boldly believed that so long as I was now in the mighty hands of Christ, I was an overcomer: "Ye are of God little children and have overcome them: because greater is he that is in you, than is in the world." 1 John 4:4.

Oh how I thanked God to have saved me from all these demonic powers from Nelly. God helped me to realize that Nelly had many dirty tricks, which she used in order to milk me of my money. She was partly responsible for all that happened to me as we spent a lot of time together. Oh I will not give my strength to this crooked lady. "Give not thy strength unto women, nor thy ways to that which destroyed kings." (pro. 31:3) I knew well that Nelly was one of the crooks who destroyed my life.

But suddenly, without notice, I was a changed person. I was free from sexually transmitted diseases and HIV/Aids. Out of the crooked generation into the chosen generation. Out of the sidelines into the witnessing platform. Suddenly no more cursing, gambling, dancing, drug addiction and alcoholism. No more discos and evil movies. No more shouting in the streets at night with my peers.

But instead I went to church to pray and praise the LORD Jesus. And the Lord brought to me heavenly joy, peace of mind and eternal love. Praise His wonderful name. Here is my song: "Holy, holy, holy is the Lord of hosts and the whole earth is full of his glory." (Isa. 6:3). There Is real meaning of life in Jesus – Hallelujah.

I allowed the scriptures to saturate my life and I could make a confession of them openly. These important things made me to exercise the act of denying myself and taking upon the nature of God. I took the character of God which enabled me to intimately fellowship with Him. In my life, I had to watch carefully not to offend my God by compromising with the world.

By faith I was able to overcome temptations victoriously, like Joseph in (Genesis 39:12). Potiphar's wife caught Joseph by his garment, "Saying lay with me; and he left his garment in her hands, and fled, and got him out." Joseph overcame sin by resisting and obeying God and fleeing by terror.

When I was filled with the Holy Spirit, the devil was very envious of me; he often tempted me by offering short-lived pleasures. But I boldly prayed in the Spirit and confessed, hardly unable to hold back my tears.

One day I remember going to bed as usual, but I could not sleep. I could hear soft incidental pop music echoing in my ears. "Point?" I asked myself. I knew these were temptations coming straight from hell. I rebuked the sounds in the name of Jesus and soon I felt peace in my soul.

Another night, the devil tempted me by bringing evil thoughts and evil dreams. In the dream I could see the picture of my former girlfriend at night, smiling, nagging, laughing and even making silly jokes to me. I could see her wearing her latest fashion garments. She looked smart, with rolled hair. In the dream I looked in surprise – Is this the African made kid who used to drive me mad at some point? I asked myself. Suddenly I woke up at night and rebuked this evil dream. I knew the devil wanted to condemn me by causing fear and doubts in my Christian life.

Fear brings defeat and fear is faith in the devil. But I resisted the devil in the name of Jesus and he fled. All the evil thoughts, evil feelings, mental pictures, bad dreams and visions which do not agree with the Word of God should be cast down by the power of the spirit of God and the word. I had power in Jesus to overcome the devil.

Therefore, after the evil temptations, I decided to write to Nelly immediately and confidently announce to her that I was saved. I knew well that it was another way of victory. I planned the note carefully being led by the spirit of God. First I'd tell her that I was saved and filled with the Holy Spirit. Secondly I would warn her sternly not to reply the letter. I confessed that I was no longer in love. I started the note with an expression of a complete victor. I wrote the testimonial note, it read: LOVE WITHOUT LUST.

Dear Nelly,

I want you to know how Gods love arrested me. Last night, I willingly surrendered my miserable life to JESUS CHRIST and I was transformed. I'm now a new creature. Jesus is my lover! His banner over me is love. I think that this letter will surprise you very much, but girl, this unconditional love has changed me, physically, mentally, and spiritually. I have decided never to be associated with you in any way whatsoever.

Nelly, I'm not crazy, but I have decided to trust Jesus as my personal savior. I'm saved and filled with the Holy Spirit. My soul is washed, sanctified and bought by the blood of Jesus Christ. I'm now God's owned property "For ye re bought with a price, therefore glorify God in your body, and in your spirit, which are God's." 1 Cor. 6:20. Read also, (1 Peter 1:18). I am not bought by silver or gold, but by the precious blood of Jesus Christ. Jesus is my savior now, the only precious one in my life. Oh how He loves me! I have forsaken all sins and evils for His sake. I will never sin again; I believe that it is Jesus alone, who can make you understand why I have made this unexpected decision. Forgive me please, if I'm very plain to you. Jesus is the only hope I have in this world now. My life is under new management.

I am now a chosen generation, a royal priest, a holy vessel and a peculiar person, that I should show forth the power and the love of Jesus Christ, who has called me out of darkness into His marvelous light. For this reasons take me as a brother in Christ and God's property. My love to you is finished. Jesus is my closest friend. His banner over me is love. Love without lust. Don't reply. Yours sincerely,

Peter N. Muya

I sealed the letter and posted it. The letter went straight to Nelly. I was sure that after breaking the seal, she would be shocked. Even today I still remember this gospel letter I wrote to Nelly and its shocking outcome. I wrote as one in heaven writing to one on earth in solemn warning and agent appeal. After reading the letter,

I was sure she would be shocked. The fear of God would fall on her, but since the purpose of writing was to glorify God's mercy and grace in my life, I had no intention of making her feel condemned. By the grace of God I wrote many letters to my friends who were strongly impressed on my mind. It took years for me to learn that God was thus indicating that another service for Him was writing Gospel letters, tracts. and books

I knew for sure that Godliness was the only thing Nelly could not imitate. There was nothing she could envy in the world, but Christianity. Her decisions were her own and so were her words. I knew that her judgments were sincere, for she considered herself unsafe, unsettled, provoked, and very much offended.

On my side, I was very careful about the world. I could not be associated with Nelly in any way. I was now a new creature. "I was the temple of the Holy Spirit." (1 Cor. 3:16-17). I knew that Nelly was of the world and I was God's owned property. Amid this crooked and mysterious world, I was saved; therefore I had to join the church where I was to be shaped, to be a Holy bride for the soon coming king, Jesus Christ. So I was now serious and I could not try to step aside for even a single moment for I knew that I could expose myself to a dangerous risk of losing my position in heaven forever. I could not play around with any girl. The Word of God commanded me to flee as though by terror from these disturbing youthful lusts "Flee also youthful lusts: but follow righteousness, faith, charity, peace, with them that call on the Lord out of a pure heart." (II Tim. 2:22).

As I read the Bible I understood God's will in my life, I began helping the pastor in organizing crusades and served in the church in many ways. I was comforted by the Word of God, which says, "Houses and riches are the inheritance of fathers, and a prudent wife is from the Lord." (Prov. 19:14). So I waited for the Lord to give me a wife. I knew to get a good and a faithful partner in this world is favor from God.

By the grace of God I was now growing strong spiritually. I was able to speak plainly to anyone about this inward change, which brought real joy and peace in my troubled life. I remember the first day I met my friend Kim in town, just some months after I was saved and filled with the Holy Spirit. I told him, "Kim, I have trusted Jesus Christ as my personal savior."

Kim looked at me for some time as though I was a ghost and with a puzzled expression he insisted ... "Are you sure, solo?" Then he lapsed into silence. Kim thought how I separated myself from the world, changed and given up my privileges within this crooked youth so as to be called a Christian. Kim thought that I was crazy. My situation must have been considered so in regard to my former life and the youthful pleasures, which I was seriously involved in.

Kim could remember how we used to climb the stairs of the nightclubs together. How we both used to drink and take drugs and once how I commanded a gang of twelve boys in town. Therefore Kim now tried to persuade me to abandon the faith, return to my former life and continue life in sin together.

In my Christian life this was one of my toughest times, because Kim asked me confusing questions which the Lord helped me to answer him. Kim's questions were demanding and I needed urgent answers. God helped me to answer all these questions with the word. In the word I had stability and an inner foundation, which held me up when my friend Kim threatened to overwhelm me. As I repeated the Word of God, I felt power and the presence of God. I felt peace as I warned Kim not to call me "Solo" again. Solo, was a nickname, which originated in the disco halls when my friends saw me twisting myself round in the manner of a wounded snake.

I told Kim the whole story of how suddenly God's love arrested me, that from midnight to sunrise all through the hours of that blessed night, I remained in bed a glowed by the power of God. I told him how I saw Jesus with His nailed hands and the scars in His ribs. And lastly, I told him how tears of joy rolled down my cheeks after laying every burden upon Jesus Christ. I told him that I trust in Jesus and I know in whom I trust.

Kim thought, compared my former life and that of a Christian, and said that I could not make it. As I told my story, glimpses of the truth came to him, but only for a moment, afterwards he begun to mock me saying that he is more righteous than me.

I left Kim and did not care what he said about me. I knew well that Kim was of the world and I was God's owned property. I was happy; I was feeling a wonderful thrill, a special feeling in my soul. I was even expecting blessed sensations of God's love to flow in my life. "Nay in all these things we are more than conquerors through him that loved us" (Rom. 8:37). I thanked God that by the power of God, I overcame all these temptations.

CHAPTER FIVE

WINNING SOULS FOR CHRIST AT HOME

SOUL WINNING IS A DIVINE Mandate In My Life. From the day I was a village teenager, I wanted to be a soul winner. Being an ordinary soul winner I believed the word of God to do the impossibilities in Jesus name. With the word I was able to kick out doubt and despair, which could make my eternal destination uncertain. My divine mandate was to win souls. Souls were my target, which kept me focused, providing me with the drive or motivation towards achieving my objectives. By pursuing my goal in life, I experienced a breakthrough in my ministry, which kept me away from predicament.

My call was to fulfill the great commission. Winning souls sparked a fire that has kept burning in my life to date. Since then I have accomplished much in soul winning which seemed to be impossible at first. This shows what an ordinary, village soul winner can do by the power of God.

My desire and zeal in my life is to make soul winning a reality. I believe with all my heart that all things are possible, in spite of a lot of opposition and ridicule from people in this world. I only require determination, persistence and aggressiveness to fight any opposing forces from the enemy, so that I could get the required breakthrough which could make me continue advancing towards my goal.

By persistently and consistently concentrating on soul winning, my ministry has grown tremendously. I will ever remain focused on soul winning. I will not allow opposition to stop me from achieving that which God has called me to do.

I was totally and unreservedly yielded to the Holy Spirit to energize me to fulfill God's plan and purpose in this final decade of destiny. I knew that for me to be very effective in my ministry, I was to receive a fresh anointing, a divine enablement for a specific purpose in my life. I knew it was God's plan for me to walk under a double portion anointing, where God's gifts and power flows through me in a wonderful way. I was now very sensitive to the leading of the Holy Spirit and I could not rely on my own talents, abilities, knowledge and experience.

I was to live a life of prayer where I could wait upon the Lord to release His anointing in my ministry. I could not rely on the past anointing, which I had received years ago. I wanted a fresh flow of His power to equip me for this end time hour. Just like King David who said, "I shall be anointed with fresh oil," (Psa. 92:10) I also believed God for the same.

In my spirit I was thirsting for this fresh oil—fresh anointing—which could make me face the challenges of life victoriously. This anointing could take me beyond my current level of experience into a new dimension of power to meet the need of desperate souls in the hour.

The Spirit made me realize that for many days I was leaning on the arm of the flesh and therefore I was quenching the flow of the Holy Spirit in my ministry. I was just trying to fulfill the work of God with my own limited strength. So I was shut out from the work of the Holy Spirit within me in the ministry. I was standing with my own agenda and not the supernatural power of God.

My heart was so grieved and I was so concerned because I knew I had fallen into a trap. I could see the spiritual condition in which I was, and I could repent and start doing God's will. My spiritual eyes were opened. The Spirit revealed to me the various areas Satan had launched the greatest attacks against me.

The devil focused his attacks in my family, my personal life and my finances. He tried to divert my attention from fulfilling the will of God so as not to reach a lost and a dying world. I thank God that the Spirit of God raised a standard against all the attacks of the enemy in my life. I was a victor and not a victim. The enemy was under my feet. In my life I knew that, in order for me to fulfill the divine mandate of winning souls, I was to be filled full time with the power from on high so that I could be able to teach other soul winners how to evangelize the world.

I could be able to share with others the greatest opportunity to win souls outside the church—out where sinners are. Reach them in their home, workplace and markets. The greatest calling for me is to lead other people to Christ. As a gospel messenger, I teach others about the urgency of this hour. One of the most eye opening verses which I taught was, "Ye have not chosen me, but I have chosen you, and ordained you that you should go and bring forth fruits and that your fruits should remain." John 15:16

Truly we are chosen, we did not choose ourselves. God chose us for a special task; we are a chosen generation called out of darkness in his marvelous light. Just as God sent Jesus into the world to fulfill His own will on earth, Jesus has chosen, called and sent us to do His will in this world. "As my father has sent me, even so I send you." (John 20:21)

I could teach Christians the importance of winning souls in their lives. By knowing the truth Christians were set free and their eyes opened. I could sound the alarm, so that they could be alert and prepare to do the will of God. I was to stop them from being involved or concerned with the problems and the cares of this life.

I could teach about the lateness of this hour and urge them to do something to reach those who are lost in sin.

We are to help those who are bound by sin, those who are desperate or hopeless and prepare them to reach out the lost with the gospel of Jesus. We have many Christians who have been lulled today into a false sense of security. They think that as long as they are attending services, they are ready to meet their Lord as he comes, without doing the will of God. Many such Christians are living under the spirit of deception, which makes them to life careless for pleasure as they follow after the world. We are called to live and do God's will.

I am a soul winner, because I believe what Jesus said, that the harvest is great. Soul winning is a divine mandate in my life. The harvest is ripe and Jesus has sent me as one of these laborers in His harvest. I am sent to reap the harvest of souls in this crooked generation before Jesus comes. I am to go out in the villages, slums, ghettos and cities in pursuit of souls. I will never allow Satan to sidetrack me and cause me to become so concerned or overwhelmed with the cares of this life, that I may fail to win the lost around me. "He that winneth souls is wise." (Prov. 11:30)

One of the most eye- opening, soul searching verses which I read every time and it sends chills up and down my spine is, "Lift up your eyes and look on the fields, they are white and ready for the harvest." (John 4:35). We are to pray and do something to be parts of this end time harvest. We are to give ourselves to reaping this harvest. "The harvest truly is great, but the laborers are few; Pray ye therefore the Lord of harvest, that he will send forth laborers into his harvest." (Matt. 9:37)

That's why I have given my life to sharing the gospel with the lost. My motto is to preach the gospel to every creature. That's why

I do appeal to our partners, sponsors, and donors to do something to support the ministry before it is too late. That's why we are training missionaries, soul winners and sending them out to fulfill the great commission.

That's why we are appealing to all Christians to volunteer to win the lost. It doesn't matter whether you have the natural abilities or your educational background, God is calling you and He is willing to accomplish His purpose with the power of the Holy Spirit in you. With the power of the Holy spirit, you have power, authority and supernatural gifts which will make you bold to do whatever He has called you to do.

God wants to release an end time outpouring of His Spirit in your life now. God's power will prepare you and equip you for a special task ahead. Be ready to receive end time anointing in this hour and you can be part of this end time harvest with Jesus. His banner over me is love.

***Soul winning is a divine mandate in my* life.**

I will lift up my eyes,
To look at the fields which are ripe for harvest,
Truly the harvest is great,
Lord, I feel passion for souls,
Let me receive a soul winners reward,
Soul winning is a divine mandate in my life.
Born to win souls for Christ,
In blessings Jesus spoke in my heart,
His voice had power with God,
To renew and revive my spirit within,
To fulfill my divine mandate,
Soul winning is a divine mandate in my life.
Jesus my heart looks to thee,

You are my example in winning souls,
For you are the greatest soul winner,
Give me a soul winners spirit,
For he that winneth soul is wise, 0
Soul winning is a divine mandate in my life.
Lord, give me power to fulfill my divine mandate,
Let your joy be full within me,
Loving Jesus, I will; live for you forever,
I will serve you all days of my life,
Till all the world will believe in you,
Soul winning is a divine mandate in my life
Lord, I live by your saving grace,
Let the streams of life flow from within,
To fill the longing souls of men,
Jesus you are the sinner's friend,
Send me out where the sinners are,
Soul winning is a divine mandate in my life.

One morning, I woke up and felt pressed in my spirit to speak about the love of God to my family around the fire. I sat next to my brothers and sisters. They were all staring at the pot of fermented porridge in the fire. Soon mother removed the pot out of fire and begun to stir it with a calabash for the purpose of cooling because of the young ones. Everyone was silently waiting for his/her share.

Suddenly father broke the silence. "Nowadays the sun is becoming too hot, that even such porridge cannot quench my thirst. Only a bottle of 'chang'aa' (Local liquor) can do me the proper cure." Father said so looking at mother to propose his motion. Mother looked at my father on the face as she was filling his cup with a gingerly and wobbling stream of porridge and she said, "In fact, we shall bury you soon, if you keep on drinking this dangerous liquor, you don't make me happy by talking like that."

Everyone was silent again. "Jesus loves you all," I said to break the silence, "Without Jesus man will never be satisfied in this world. Jesus is the only drink that can quench the thirst in every man of whatever race or station in life." Father looked at me as though the words were tearing the inside of his being and he went to drink chang'aa without saying a word.

At home, I normally sat beside the fire, reading the Bible and talking about heaven at every given opportunity. Let me say that this was rather a very surprising spectacle to my family who were not believers and mostly to my father, Muya, who carried long sullen moods.

My father was a short, notorious village elder with crooked ways of life. He lived recklessly and drank far too much. He would not leave the pub till late at night. In fact, it is not an exaggeration to say that he did not wear a pair of shoes in his life, but he was drinking all day long. His dear wife, Veronicah Nyambura, my mother, had long ago deserted the evil ways and embraced religion.

Mother was plump, and liked tea a lot. Her bitter moment came when she learned that her loving husband was in the hands of the police, having been arrested for being a drunkard and disorderly. It seemed fateful that my father was a failure in life, yet it must be said that mother was kind and obeyed him as her husband. She could be heard rebuking neighbors and relatives who tried to create curiosity and family wrangle by alleging that her husband was a perpetual drunkard.

Since the change in me had been so sudden for my family to conceive, they thought that I was somehow crazy. Not only were they disturbed about me, but they were also frightened by the probability of having a nut in the family. In spite of all my reasoning's from the Bible showing them the great advantage of knowing Christ as my savior, they still remained aloof of my convictions.

I am glad to say my testimony has reversed the bad ways of life in my family. Praise the Lord! I'm sure that my mother and her other children who are not saved will soon grasp the impact in this faith in Jesus Christ. Also I believe that before the second coming of Christ everybody in my family will experience this wonderful love of Jesus. I also praised the Lord that even my father who at first was a bitter opposer of my testimony asked for a Bible to read in his spare time. But unfortunately he died suddenly, having no hope of eternal life. When preachers and Christians persuaded him to repent he promised that he would repent "tomorrow." But alas! Tomorrow never comes!

My father was an alcoholic and, although alcohol had destroyed his life, he could not stop drinking. He could not believe in God even the day he was suffering and in severe pain in his bed at Kenyatta National Hospital where he was admitted with acute kidney failure. The doctors tried hard to save his life to no avail. So they discharged him and after a week he peacefully died at home.

My father was gone, never to be seen again in this world. He died a miserable sinner. Mother had left him beside the fire, warming and listening to the radio as she went to bed. But she was surprised to wake up and see him dead on the ground. She gazed at the dark-brown coat which my father had worn with disbelief. That night my younger sister slept in the opposite room when mother touched her with a trembling hand and woke her up. They put the body on his bed.

My brother and I slept in a separate house some meters away from my father's house. But when the news of my father's death reached us, I fell into depression. Seeking help and comfort, I consulted my elder brother, who listened gravely as I poured out the grief on his shoulder.

My God spoke to me through the Spirit and said, "It is time for you to turn away from earthly grief's and seek eternal blessing." The Spirit convinced me of eternal peace in Jesus Christ. That peace must be immaculate; a single error would render it unfit for use. But that perfect peace is valued in my life above all worldly things.

But real shock gripped my heart when I looked at my father's dead body, with its smooth black face. He died suddenly before the day he called tomorrow. I looked again at my father. He was wrapped in a blanket in his bed. "Is this the same father who had been so full of laughter last night after we had a cup of tea together before going to bed?" I shuddered inwardly. I said in my heart, No, this is just a cold dead shell I'm looking at with a dull face.

My family joined me in loud mourning then. But where is that living personality which had evidently vacated that unbruised body. I shuddered again at the answer to that question. Never in life could this awful moment have been so real to me as I looked down to my father's dead body. He was at the dead's party and I was fully convinced that soon or later I was also waiting this awful call whether I liked it or not.

All my brothers and sisters and relatives were called in. My father's family was also summoned. Amos was my father's youngest brother, the only closest member of his family. Both were born in a family of five in Ngecha village, Limuru. They all went to school together and later my father left school and announced to his tearful parents that he was going to Rift Valley Province at Nakuru town to seek for employment. In 1950, my father got married to mother as a second wife. The following year they were blessed with a beautiful daughter. Amos, my father's brother, traveled periodically to Nakuru with presents of cassava to make him return home according to traditional belief. But he could not. He lived in the Rift Valley until his death.

Before the family and the relatives came, my sister Wanjiru, who is a devoted Christian, gave us moral support. She brought a group of pious youth who produced a perfect work of praising the Lord. Each night they brought the drums, and my sister selected the finest chorus, which touched everybody in my family. She turned our mourning into joy. In our family we are taught to praise God for all things, just as the Bible implores on Christians to rejoice always.

After three days of grief, everybody in my extended family was present in our home, ready to escort their departed kin to his last resting place. I imagined Dad teetering on the brink of eternal ruin... Poor Dad, I wish you knew that your death was so near and that God is real. You would have confessed your sins, but now it was too late. Good-bye, Dad! I said inwardly as I paid my last respects to my father.

Jesus sustained me in His power to overcome this moment of grief. If I had been lying there like my father I knew that for sure I would have gone straight to heaven. But my father's testimony was so plain. He lived as a drunkard and eventually died a drunkard. Which fool could not read the Bible and then know the fate about my father at once? No amount of sprinkled water nor our petitions could change his destiny. Only Him alone was able to answer for his deeds when the judgement day comes.

This event changed everything in my family. But God assured me that my life was hidden in Jesus Christ. So there was no need to fear death. "And I heard a voice from heavens saying unto me. Write, blessed are the dead, which die in the Lord from henceforth: Yea, saith the spirit that they may rest from their labours; and their work do follow them." (Rev. 14:13)

Jesus is my savior and He also provides everything in my life. He is above my joy. "His name is love. Precious in the sight of the Lord is the death of his saints." (Psa. 116:15). My dear friend, let me say that I can cover sheets and sheets of papers but yet I cannot write even a half of what I feel. My joy no human can tell.

"The joy of the Lord is my strength." (Neh. 8:10). I became young.

CHAPTER SIX

LUST IS NOT LOVE

IN MY LIFE, I LIKE to tell my real story of how God's sacrificial love arrested me. I do teach the youth on how to differentiate the lustful love of the flesh and God's redemptive love. I joyfully give them tips on how to overcome peer pressure by obeying the word of God, living a holy life and chilling out from sexual lusts.

I was a drug addict and a fornicator, but when I received Jesus Christ as my personal savior, I was transformed. I obtained a new life that was very different from that of the world. It was not a self-planned experience, yet it affected me all over, mentally, spiritually and physically.

This unconditional love went beyond the confines of my girlfriend Nelly, Family and personal interests. I call this kind of love, Love without lust for it affected every fiber of my being and I was completely changed. To my former girlfriend Nelly and my closest Friend Kim they looked upon me as a stricken Buffalo that had left the herd. I knew that I was set free from the lustful love of the world, but I did not know how I could tell them how it happened.

God helped them to know that I was a changed person who was delivered out of this crooked generation into the chosen generation. I was set free, suddenly, no more illicit sex, no more abusing drugs, no more illicit brews and discos. In the village church, I helped my pastor to witness and together we were winning souls for Christ as never before.

The purpose of writing this book is to reach the youth and persuade them to escape from lustful love of the world and help them find God's redemptive love before they perish in hell. Many students in our learning institutions are suffering from mental illness, including stress or depression. Stress has many risks and can trigger a huge number of health problems.

In my interview with some students, they told me that victims of drug abuse eat too much food, over sleep, drink illicit brews and become very violent. These increased evil behaviors in the body can cause fear and other emotions that might lead to depressions. As a pastoral counselor, I have a positive way to deal with the victims by helping them find a workable solution, which includes a change of attitude. Another thing I do is to lead the victims to seek help from God through prayer. The bible encourages' "I call to you in times of trouble, because you will answer me "Psalms.88.7. Vic tums of drug abuse are lured by their bodies to engage into illicit sex, which results into unwanted pregnancies and abortions.

Valentine's day is the evil day when they meet to celebrate their lustful love in all forms, including engaging in illicit sex. You will meet them in the streets buying flowers for their girlfriends and paying for having sex in the hotel rooms. If you are looking for real love that is lasting, call Jesus Christ to save you from evil behaviors.

What is lust? It is a very strong desire to have or get something. Many people in this hurting world are having a strong lust for power, fame and wealth. Women are having a strong lust for beauty, while the youth are having a very strong lust for illicit sex. That's why we have unwanted pregnancies and abortions.

The bible warns about lust.' But each person is tempted when he is lured and enticed by his own lust. Then lust when it has conceived gives birth to sin, and sin when it is fully grown brings forth death" (James 1:14-15)

God's love is redemptive " But God shows his Love for us in that, while we were still sinners, Christ died for us all" (Romans 5:8) A glance of faith at the Calvary marks on Christs body will silence your every excuse, your sins of refusing a free pardon at the cost of the savior's blood will sink you into eternal death in Hell forever.

That's why Paul told the young Timothy' 'Flee sexual lusts, pursue righteousness, faith, love and peace" (2 Timothy 2-22) He also warned him to "Abstain, from Fornication" (2 Thessalonians 4-3)

I teach on total abstinence from illicit sex and waiting until the wedding day. My topic with the youth include positive living, Behavioral change, God is love, Love without Lust. I'm called to help the youth to discover God's redemptive love. This agape love is what I call, Love Without Lust. It helps the youth to live together in the church without having sex until the wedding day.

My missions to preach the gospel to all people, Including the youth. "woe to me if I don't preach the gospel" (2 Corinthians 9-16)

Nowadays in the universities and other institutions of higher learning drug abuse or alcoholism has become the most serious problem which is causing murder and suicide to our students. Students say that they are drinking or abusing drugs for fun, others want to show off or relieve their tensions. Others drink or abuse the drugs to forget their worries or escape from reality.

Unfortunately, when the student is hooked by drugs or alcohol, he /she becomes an addict. Addiction is a relapsing condition a problem with an underlying cause students who are affected by this addictive condition have difficulties in achieving life expectancy, goals, visions, therefore the victim cannot establish sustainable development including academic development. Many students fail their examinations and are unable to practice the skills which they acquired in the university or college due to this problem of addiction.

I have rescued some students from addiction through my pastoral counseling, some others are healed from their health problems which affected their mental health and some organs in their bodies.

One university student vowed to give up drinking and abusing drugs. Therefore, he passed examination because he was sober. Eventually, he joined the church and could not be hooked again, he succumbed to drugs and he walked with good friends.

That's why I am teaching the youth the word of God. "Abstain from every form of evil. Now may the God of peace himself sanctify you completely and may your whole spirit, soul and body be preserved blameless at the coming of our lord Jesus Christ. He who calls you is faithful; he will also do it" (2Thess-5-22-24)

I am working to see that the word of God sanctifies our students in the body, soul and spirit. Our students are engaging themselves in toxic relationships which are causing them to kill their partners after betrayal and making them commit suicide.

Drug abuse is causing students to lose self-control or inhibition or the ability to make sound decisions. That's why they engage in embarrassing, heinous acts like Killing or committing suicide.

Intoxication demises your perception which is risky. In this poor state of mind, you can easily be engaged into destructive behaviors like crime or murder. It gives the victim a false belief of enhanced " high " mood or courage which leads to risky decisions like murder and suicide.

Drug abuse has caused students to involve themselves in causal relationship and others are sleeping around with multiple sex partners. They are engaging in unprotected sexual activities in exchange for money. That's why we have many victims of HIV/AIDS in our universities and colleges this day.

As a youth counselor I am, teaching them how to overcome peer pressure, drug abuse and fornication. Many families are crying foul because of the death of their loved ones, which was influenced by a toxic lover or drug abuse.

I remember that recently I was sitting watching television when the presenter narrated a very horrifying episode of a 20-year-old JKUAT 3rd Year student Rita who was murdered in Roysambu on Sunday, January 14, 2024.A few days later the detectives were probing the murder case which led to the apprehension of two Nigerians who were suspected to have committed this heinous act. They also discovered the victims head in a dam.

One month before this murder we had another brutal murder of 24 old girl, Starlet Wahu Mwangi by a toxic lover and a serial killer John Ongoa Matara in south C estate in Nairobi. More victims emerged to write the statements of assault and attempts of murder by the same toxic lover and serial killer.

When the world is moving too fast I am busy rescuing youth from the dangers of navigating through the craziest modest body image, media internet and many evil things that are trapping them in these evil days. The youth and especially university students are acknowledging the social consequences of assault, sex abuse and murder.

Today's information communication and technology (ICT) bombards with the youth causing sex-abuse, drug abuse and the spread of HIV/AIDS in the world. Although development is achieved through ICT, indeed confusion seems to characterize it, as the youth has hailed it as their most significant achievement.

However, one should not be blind to the challenges or even the hazards that (ICT) poses to the human race, especially to our youth in the whole world. Unfortunately using mobile phone is making the internet to be a highway of evil behaviors, such as fraud, terrorism, pornography, fornication, drug abuse, illegal trade and murder.

With biblically based information I am rescuing the youth and helping them tackle life challenges by teaching them Godly ways on dating, courtship, how to overcome peer pressure and other evil behaviors. I have helped many youths to crossover from this crooked generation into a chosen generation, into the Kingdom of God.

After teaching them in our youth seminars many are fleeing from fornication, drug abuse and other evil behaviors. I am telling them that the devil comes to steal kill and destroy (John 10-10). The devil doesn't care how many degrees you could be having he will plan to kill or destroy you. Declare to the devil- "Kill me not!"

Avoid Toxic Lovers In The Social Media

The devil has trapped millions of our youth when they are surfing or browsing in the internet or YouTube using their smartphones. You find them addicted to staring at naked pictures of ladies or nude men in the internet or YouTube.

I am talking to the youth in the colleges of higher learning to avoid toxic lovers or relationships that could trap them in the social media. These toxic lovers are promising our girls benefits of fulfilling love making affair and as they rush expecting favors, they are murdered.

This toxic lover is very selfish, inconsiderate, self-centered and very brutal. Thus therefore asking our girls to double check love influences or traits of those you are looking to be associated with them on the social media.

My take is don't accept strangers because you'd land on a toxic lover even if he promises you heaven, money or any favors. Be careful and don't surround yourself with toxic lovers. Who could be taking advantage of your generosity or beauty. Please avoid these evil behaviors.

With the bible I teach the youth how they can interact with the opposite sex without fornication. I help them how to overcome watching harmful images of pornography and filthy videos in the internet.

I make sure that the word of God sinks deep in their hearts. It's the word of God which delivers, saves, purifies, builds, strengthens, informs, motives, equips and enlightens the youth. I guide them through the word in the proper ways to marriage with hot-button topics on dating, purity, self-esteem, emotions, faith and righteousness.

These Godly topics are designed to help the youth to better understand themselves and their body development. I tell them how God cares about every aspect of their lives. I encourage them to say No! to evil behaviors and how to say Yes! to Jesus Christ our savior and redeemer.

There is a very common adage that "whoever captures the youth will have the future". That's why the greatest world dictator called 'Hitler' captured the youth and used them do evil works of killing the Jews for twelve Years.

National leaders and even politicians have been promising the youth better life opportunities which could provide social welfare, but they have been waiting until today. Even the devil knows how to use the youth to destroy or kill others.

Many Psychologists are teaching our youth on how to live with good behaviors in our colleges of higher learning, but after the seminars the youth continue to burn properties, abuse drugs and consume alcohol. The best weapon that we can all use to help our youth to overcome peer pressure and evil behaviors is the word of God.

I am teaching the youth how to differentiate God's love with lust. Lust is not Love. Because of not knowing the difference many of our youth are ending up in toxic relationships. I teach the youth the importance of taking time to know your lover and his/her background. There is an adage that "when the deal is too good think twice."

Think twice before engaging into any relationship. I tell Christians in our youth conference or Convection not to allow your lover in your small house. Don't walk with your lover in a secret place alone, because your emotions could lead to sin and mostly fornication.

Abstain From Fornication

Jane was a faithful Christian in our church in Nairobi, one day she broke her cordial rule of not allowing any lover into her tiny room. Her lover asked to know where she was living. The lady said in her heart that, "Let me take my lover where I'm living". She invited him in her house for lunch.

In the house she switched on her favorite gospel music as she cooked lunch. As they waited the guy started touching and kissing her soon as the joke went on and on, The guy pulled down her pants and he pulled out his trouser. They were burning with passion and their emotions were very high. The lady spread apart her legs and the guy went through and the game began.

Later they both blamed each other for what had happened. The next morning the girl narrated the whole story to her pastor and although she was restored she could not erase those evil memories in her mind. The pastor advised her to make hard decisions of changing and blocking the toxic lover. She was told to call the police if the lover threatened her. Please avoid these toxic lovers, you will cry foul.

If you are a student be very careful because university hostels have been turned into criminal and prostitution dens. They have become hideouts and convergence points for criminals. There are all sorts of evil behaviors including prostitution and increased cases of organized crimes.

Thika Town for example is the home of several middle level colleges and a few universities. Consequently, the town has seen a boom of youngsters seeking college education. However, some of these students are not in this town for education only. Many have turned into crime, peddling drugs, prostitution among others.

Let me try to focus on prostitution. You will find some female students on the streets of our towns and cities hawking sex for money instead of them concentrating in their studies. Other students are in what they call in the universities, "sponsorship" relationships. This is what I'm Calling Toxic Love affair. The worst thing is that this relationship will end up with frustrations a and the lover will be dumped. Victims of these evil relationship cry foul after they are abused, dumped or murdered by their lovers.

During the sponsorship relationships you will meet several female students walking with their toxic lover's shoulder high from one big club to another exposing their breasts and thighs. They turn to prostitution when they are dumped by their toxic lovers to maintain their high standard life-styles.

This kind of love is destroying our students because it's based on money and material things in exchange of sex. That's why you meet with female students flocking in the streets trying to hook toxic lovers, while others engage into commercial sex. Many people especially the rich or politicians are mostly caught up in the trap of sponsors by female students.

This is making prostitution to be a good business for female students. This illegal business is shooting up at an alarming speed in our institutions of higher learning. One wonders why a beautiful female student can manage to be a sex worker for money.

In the other hand, male students have turned to wealth women sponsors who will buy them laptops, phones and other goodies in exchange of sex. This sugar mummies select their target male students very carefully. And because they know many male students are very low financially, they strike a deal with male students for sex. Many male students have fallen in the trap of sex with sugar mummies for money. Later the male students will realize how stupid they have been after they are milked all their strength.

It's very funny to note that some students in this institutions do not know whether this illegal business for both male and female students' exist because they are very busy concentrating on their studies. But they are suspicious when they see some male and female students with huge sums of money which they don't get from HELB or from their parents.

University leaders must stop ignoring the plight of the growing number of students who are turning to be sex workers and start offering counseling or send us to rescue students through our counseling services. The rising living costs, higher student's fees, together with access to the internet or social media has contributed to evil behavior in the universities.

I have said that prostitution has been there in the universities for decades although there are no obvious statistics because it is a hidden business. All students who do these illegal business dress fashionably and you will see them using expensive laptops and smartphones. The use of social networks in bringing prostitution and heinous acts in our universities and colleges. The bible says –For this is the will of God, your sanctification: that you should abstain from fornication (2 Thess:4-3)

Media reports have recently featured stories of university students who have died in tragic circumstances. Some were killed by the toxic lovers; Some other Students were reported lost but later they were found dead under unclear circumstances.

Clearly there is a silent crisis unbounding within our universities student's community. This crisis is duly recognized for what it is and measures should be implemented to address it. These many social problems in our colleges are caused by peer pressure in our students who are facing huge challenges in adapting to changing demands in their lives.

Soured Relationships

These increased social problems and evil behaviors impact on the mental health of our youth, making them lose the power to withstand peer influence which makes them lose their sense of focus in life.

Our university students need pastoral counseling and social support programs which can help them overcome these soured relationships which have been a common trend in our colleges. These toxic relationships are causing brutal and premature deaths.

I have seen many students suffering from these increased soured relationships.

A few years ago, students at the university of Nairobi were left speechless when one of their own, Kevin Ikatwa was found murdered in cold blood in his rented house in Kangemi Nairobi. His girlfriend was arrested for the murder that took place at his rented house.

Elsewhere, a 24-year-old Sharon Achieng, a student at Mount Kenya University was found dead at a house she had decided to rent in an estate in Nakuru. A lot of things happen to students in the name of toxic relationships or "come we stay" relationships in the campuses.

One of the most recent cases involving love gone sour among lovers was the case of Elmond Ruto of Egerton University who stabbed his girlfriend to death before attempting suicide. He killed Cynthia Chelagat after they had a conflict in Njokerio, Njoro outside the university.

During Investigations it emerged that his girlfriend had complained to her friends that her toxic relationship with Ruto was in trouble. Her landlord said there had been frequent scuffles between the two.

Nowadays, University students are increasingly becoming victims or perpetrators of murder as hostels have become dens of criminals where everything like selling of drugs, Prostitution and even organized theft is done after drinking the illicit brews openly.

University students have become an easy target for criminals and they are vulnerable to crime to cater for their financial frustration. Many students who are at their twenties feel that they have nothing to lose even if they are caught by the police for crime. They want to live in rented houses so that they can live together with student lovers. This evil behavior is very common and it is trending in our campuses although it's out of order.

The students are boasting saying- "This is our time to experiment, adventure and enjoy ourselves." Our students are risk takers and they want to live in fornication mood in their residential areas. That's where they engage in make shift marriages, come we stay or co-habiting. Yet they both remain college going students with toxic relationships which is casual and very risky.

This evil behavior leaves the parents confused and frustrated for they don't know what is going on in the campuses. They don't know how the students die in the universities in unclear circumstances, others are vulnerable to emotional and psychological scars that arise from experiencing evil behaviors that they were not adequately prepared for.

• • • •

THE POWER OF PASTORAL Counseling

As a parent and a pastor I should ask all the authorities concerned to allow us to help the students with pastoral counseling before they perish. We can volunteer to guide them spiritually; with the word of God. We are tired of hearing heinous acts by students every day.

A university student in Masai Mara University was murdered outside the bar where he was drinking. Another student Emily Ngetich was found dead in her rented apartment in Manyatta estate Narok County. She was raped before she was killed by her colleague a student from Moi University.

Atieno Ondingo, a student in Maasai mara University was found outside the campus hostel under unclear circumstances after visiting the washroom. When she was rushed to Narok Hospital, she was pronounced dead.

Another student in the same college died after collapsing in his rented room at Total Estate in Narok County, it was not clear what Killed Kirui. Mercy Keino a university student was found dead after a party in Waiyaki way, Westlands, Nairobi.

As a youth Counselor I have a few tips on how to overcome peer pressure which is disturbing our students. I encourage them to face reality and receive Jesus Christ as their personal savior. Jesus has power to save deliver and redeem you from sins, bondage and addictions.

My Testimony

I do give the youth my personal testimony of how I was a drug addict and fornicator, but when I surrendered my miserable life to Jesus, I was transformed. After growing up spiritually in the church, it was a sunny morning on early February 1985, when I decided to find a soulmate. I wrote a love letter to Mary Gathoni proposing her as my life partner. I admired her good behavior as we were fellowshipping with her in the Full Gospel Church Kiambogo Village, Gilgil Sub county.

I had known her for more than two years and her Christian behavior made me to be convinced that she was fit to be my life partner. I loved and admired her wonderful singing voice. I had all the signs that proved that she was fit for me. When I gave her the letter of my proposal I was trembling with excitement. Although I was anxiously waiting for her positive response, I was wondering whether my proposal will be entertained.

We continued to meet in the Church meetings and fellowships. After one month she had not replied the letter. She Kept talking to me until she could not hold back her feelings. After doing her own research she discovered that we were compatible and she joyfully replied the letter positively.

Our Courtship started and Four years later, I approached the leaders of the local church and I told them my story. They appreciated my intentions because I was a full time pastor in one of their branches.

The church leaders, my friends, neighbors and family members organized a very colorful wedding and after paying the dowry by the help of the senior pastor. I was given the date for the wedding. Praise the LORD.

With the assistance of a very supportive committee from the church who were working hard, We Were joyfully walking through the aisle towards the altar to exchanged marriage vows at the full Gospel Church Kiambogo Church on 23rd November 1990. After the sermon, the presiding minister with a group of other ministers present prayed for us. Family members, relatives, and friends, encouraged and gave us gifts.

As a pastor, I was busy in the ministry, but I still ensured that I had quality time with my wife. Even though I was a Pentecost pastor, I made sure that I was not carried away by the revival waves and neglect my family. The holy spirit reminded me always to be at home early to meet my wife's spiritual and physical needs.

My wife and children are my life and I would not want to neglect them because of my work. Together with my wife we grew up spiritually by attending couples' seminars in the church. Our lives became relaxed and inspiring. Even today we have learnt how to live in harmony and even though we do disagree, we have known how to resolve our differences amicably.

We don't fear challenges or disagreements because God has helped our children to have their own families and it so much fun to live together without our children. Our Children are adults who are working in different parts of Kenya with their families. with my wife we have enjoyed many anniversaries and solved our challenges together. We are praying for our children and grandchildren every day.

My friend I want to help you to come out from toxic relationship. This is what is trending in the social media. This is affecting many youth's reputation and its devastating. Please, I don't want you to be labeled by your friend as a toxic lover simply because he/she does not want a relationship.

It's bad to judge the book by its cover, read the content first. Not all relationships are toxic. A true lover Will not ask for sex first before marriage, he will show seriousness to marry you by going to meet your parents and pay dowry. As the word says, "Therefore man shall leave his Father and Mother and hold fast to his wife and the two shall become one flesh." (Ephesians 5-31). This will be your best time to enjoy sex for the first time. Lust will lead you to sex before marriage which is fornication.

Fornication will make your partner to never trust you as a husband or wife. Why do you trust God to lead you to your husband or wife, instead of hanging on with toxic lovers and destroy your body.. I want you to start a faithful marriage relationship which will be without tears later, Call Jesus Christ to save you and he will lead you to your life partner.

Remember that Gods plan is to deliver you from the powers of darkness. But the devils plan is to steal, kill and destroy (John 10-10) So declare to the devil – 'KILL ME NOT' Read my latest book. **#Kill Me Not!** #

CHAPTER SEVEN

A POWER PACKED SOUL WINNER

IN MY CHRISTIAN LIFE there have been trials, temptations and tragedies, but I thank God for He has brought me through all of them. The infilling of the Holy Spirit that I received made me to be strong in the Lord. The Holy Spirit has helped me to grow up spiritually and has made me to move on from glory to glory. Where the Spirit is, there is power and liberty.

I have confident assurance of God's protection in my life, which enabled me to remain calm through all the circumstances of life. I thank God that Jesus has promised to be with me throughout my life. That's why I represent Him here on earth. There is no greater honor on earth than that of working with Jesus as His ambassador. The spirit of God creates a passion in my heart, which Satan cannot extinguish.

In spite of the severe testing, failures and discouragements, I have never had another passion in my life as strong as that of living and serving God under the spirit's anointing. There is no greater joy and satisfaction than that of being used by God in any capacity whatsoever. I'm always more than willing to speak about God in any place or circumstance. In my life preaching is very important.

I'm glad that I keep my eyes firmly fixed on the source of power – Jesus Christ. Rom. 8:31-35. "What shall we then say to these things? If God be for us, who can be against us? He that spared not his own son, but delivered him up for us all, how shall He not with Him also freely give us all things? Who shall lay anything to the charge of God's elect? It is God that justifieth. Who is he that condemns? It is Christ that died, yea rather, that is risen again, who is even at the right hand of God, who also makes intercession for us. Who shall separate us from the love of Christ? Shall tribulation, or distress, or persecution, or famine, or nakedness, or peril or sword?"

There is one source of inspiration from which in particular I derived a fire, which made it possible for me to be a power packed gospel messenger. I first received guidance from the teachings of Rev. T.L. Osborn and his wife in a soul-winner's seminar in Nakuru town. He had a big crusade and later he taught in a seminar in a big tent. His words were anointed which I will remember as long as I live, and I hope you will also. "I am an ambassador of Christ. I am more than extraordinary; I am what God says I am. I can do what God says I can."

After the seminar these words were still ringing in my heart and T.L. Osborn kept teaching me through the mail. He also sent me a supply of soul winning and faith building books, sermon tapes and tracts. As I read the books and listened to the tapes, the zeal of God begun to consume me. It kept burning in my soul. There was a driving force in my spirit, and a fire that couldn't be quenched.

My soul was moved by great love for the lost world. It was a time for me as an ambassador of Christ to stop floundering around being generally preoccupied with my own agenda and problems, but I was to move on in faith to make a difference in this hurting world. I am glad to say that the efforts made by the late T.L. Osborn and his wife to teach and encourage me were not in vain. His teachings have changed the whole of Africa. Today "Africa is for Jesus." We have now a powerful gospel mission of reaching the rest of Africa with the gospel of love.

Also in my life I have been telling God to take me into unprecedented manifestation of his word through the teachings of the late Morris Cerullo, which makes me to be bold to continue with my vision. I have another inspiration from the late R.W. Schambach, who is both my friend and my critic. I thank God for the prayers of these men of God and the power they have imparted in my life and ministry. They have revived me to touch many lives, through their powerful and life changing teachings. It is my prayer that God will bless their ministries and families.

I depended entirely upon God for daily spiritual upkeep and so I became a young power-packed gospel messenger. I was a very effective soul-winner. I was also very pleased to work hand in hand with various gospel ministry organizations around the world. My burden is to obey God's command, which is to preach the gospel to every creature on earth. My vision is "Reaching Africa for Jesus." For many years in this fruitful ministry I have come to know the answer to the many questions which had long troubled me before I got saved. I will bless the Holy Spirit for coming into my new heart.

I will bless the day I was born again. I will bless my ministry. I will bless the angels for becoming faithful guardians in my life. I will thank the Lord very much for blessing me in a wonderful way. "Oh what a great change—out of being a hopeless charcoal burner into a power-packed gospel messenger." Praise the Lord. After waiting upon the Lord, I'm glad to let you know that I was blessed with a beautiful lady who is my wife today. We are also blessed with two daughters and a son. "He who finds a wife finds a good thing, and obtains favor from the LORD." (Pro. 18:22). "Your wife will be like a fruitful vine within your house, your children will be like olive shoots around your table." (Psa. 128:3). I am not proud about the past, but I must speak plainly to everybody about this wonderful experience, which brought an inward peace and love from God which has been an anchor of the glorious hope of Jesus in me.

I have a consuming desire to preach the gospel and I am deeply convicted that God has called me to the ministry. I'm a full time pastor who has surrendered his life to the ministry. By the love of God in my life, I have discovered the answer to the main question, which had long troubled me: why was I born? I was born to preach the gospel, to reach Africa for Jesus. Praise the Lord! "Where there is no vision, the people perish." (Proverbs 29:18).

As I use my special abilities in God's work, He is quick to respond confirming His promises with miracles and wonders. To me it is great to serve this wonderful God. I truly consider it a great privilege to be His ambassador and let Him reach others through me in Africa. Has He not filled me with the Holy Spirit and told me personally, "Fear not, I am Jesus?" Yes! And I will serve and love Him with all my strength. Jesus is my closest friend. "You are my friends, if you do whatsoever I command you." (John 15:14).

I do not always understand how God performs miracles, but I rejoice when His love brings about transformation of souls and bodies. I very much appreciate and love our ministry because through it and other ministries I am brought up spiritually. I like writing tracts because it is wonderful. I write testimonies of what the Lord is doing in my life today. God has opened doors for me, that many of my tracts are preaching to thousands and possibly to millions, in this country and overseas. I have had requests from many lands with reports of blessings. It is a ministry that requires steadfast faith, for when you write a tract, few people write to thank you for a tract that has blessed them. I thank God that He has encouraged me to write. "He that winneth souls is wise." (Prov. 15:14).

Jesus is my hope. "Now the God of hope fill you with all joy and peace in believing that ye may abound in hope, through the power of the Holy Ghost," (Romans 15:13). Thank you Jesus for being my closest friend. My hope is built on nothing else but Christ. I dare not trust in any false hope but lean on Jesus the solid rock of all ages.

Question: Have you made this commitment of faith to Jesus Christ? God is always calling you into His kingdom: "Come unto me all ye that labor and are heavy laden and I will give you rest." (Matt. 11:28). Jesus will deliver you from all such things, like riots, evil demonstrations, threats, murder, suicide, sex-perversion, drug addiction, jealousy, pride, disease and alcoholism. The Bible says: "He that covers his sins shall not prosper but whosoever confesses and forsakes them shall have mercy." (Pro. 28:13).

The world today is in the hands of a demon-inspired youth who seem to drag it down to degradation and damnation. The reason why the Bible says: "Rejoice, O young man, in thy youth and let they heart cheer thee in the days of thy youth and the sight of thine eyes: but know thou, that for all these things God will bring thee into judgement," (Ecc. 11:9).

My dear friend, respond to God's calling right now for He is standing at the door of your heart now, waiting for you to open for Him. Will you? Why are you afraid to say before your Lord and creator, "I'M SORRY LORD." For sure you will experience another moving power that will cause you to say, "Thank you LORD!"

Jesus will conquer all your negative thoughts and make you a completely new person, as you would like to be. His name is love! "But God commends His love towards us in that while we were still sinners, Christ died for us!" (Rom: 8).

My friend, God loves you very much and so do I. It is my prayer that God's love in Jesus Christ will be manifested in your life and therefore, you will become a completely new person. As God desires it for us.

For more help write soon for I am always ready and prepared to take the Gospel everywhere. My prayer is, "Lord, make the nations my heritage and the ends of the earth my possession." (Psa. 2:8).

Finally, after a long struggle, I have surrendered my life to the ministry. I am glad that the Lord meets all my financial needs. I will joyfully represent Him here on earth and do His words. "Behold, I will send my messenger." (Mark 1:2)

My mission is to loose children of God of the hands of wickedness, to undo the heavy burdens, let the oppressed go free and break every yoke of the enemy. (Isaiah 5:6) I distribute gospel tracts to schools, public places, hotels, bars, disco-halls, universities, colleges, hospitals, cinema-halls and nightclubs. My motto is to preach the gospel to every creature. We are sent messengers of God to preach the gospel to every creature in this world. Let your prayer be, "Lord make me a gospel messenger for you." Believe in the Lord your God, and you shall be established; believe His prophets, and you shall prosper," (II Chronicles 20:20).

Called To win Souls for Christ

Yes! I was called to win souls for Christ
The silent kid which love assails
Walks daily in the valleys of love eternal
Where I feel love winds rattling
And eternal rivers running fast in my heart
Lord! In me thy love impact in Africa
In amusing honor all men could hear the cry
Called to win souls for Christ
Great happiness is found in me

While crying for the souls of men
I sang my praises in the open
My joys from Jesus Christ flowed
Eternal life is found in Him
The peace they seek is also in Him In Africa the blessed kid
stood still
When I'm weak I'm strong
When my strength and self fails
The LORD my Savior prevails
I will fast and pray
For the souls of men in Africa
Raised as modern prophet
With heavenly visions and goals Called to win souls for
Christ
Lord before thy cross I kneel
Fill my craving heart with love
And a deep burning flame for souls
With a mighty anointing baptize me
Teach me thy great work of soul winning
Let me be a soul winner here on earth
And go with thee in the entire world to win souls
Called to win souls for Christ

CHAPTER EIGHT

HOW GODS LOVE ARRESTED ME

AFTER MY SALVATION, I continued to read the Bible and to meditate on God's word. I became used to enjoying the fellowship and the presence of God in my life. A fire of God's love began to burn in my soul. I would not be ashamed to speak about the love of God in my life. I was a victor in the world's battlefields. God's love casts out fear. (1 John 4:18) Jesus is my lover.

One day, the morning was sharp and clear; it was about noon, and upon the south of the slant hill was our home, which was surrounded with a fence. The sky was pure blue, without a cloud or a speck. Under the trees one could clearly see me seated and singing one of my favorite gospel songs in my native language, "Ngai ni wendo"—meaning 'God is love'.

The atmosphere was cool and still, just what I needed for study. There was such calm accompanied by soft sounds made by insects. With a New Testament in my hand, I was quietly meditating upon some scripture readings. I meditated upon the word of God for hours. These words were the source of blessing in my life. I learnt that the Bible was written to inspire, warn and instruct me. I took the word as food for my life.

As I read the word of God, Calvary love broke in my heart with surprising consciousness. I looked again at the word of God: "But God commands his love towards us in that while we were still sinners Christ died for us." (Rom. 5:8) I understood the nature and the character of God. I knew that it's by God's love that I was saved. God's love is steadfast and everlasting. "The Lord hath appeared of old unto me saying, yea, I have loved thee with an everlasting love: therefore with loving-kindness have I drawn thee." (Jeremiah 31:3)

Love is a short word, but it had a deep meaning in my life. To me, it was more than a word. It was an attitude, which involved my whole being. God's love affected my dealings; hence, I knew that everything that I have in my life is a gift from Him. This includes my salvation, the Holy Spirit, and all other blessings, which I have received from Him by faith. I learnt that I was made in the image of God. And I promised to follow Him in love and love in deed. You might be contemplating about your feelings right now. So what is love?

Love is an English word, which has various expressions. You need to experience it practically so as to understand it clearly. Love has life like a seed, and when it is planted in you, it develops slowly and gradually. For example, when you think of someone else more than you do of yourself, you are falling in love. Therefore, love is a feeling of great friendliness.

Love Is Strong As Death

Before my salvation I lived in sin and, after every act of sin, I felt guilty and condemned by the devil. Naturally to me, sin was a way of life; I was in total darkness amongst my perishing generation. But before I was lost forever, God's love arrested me "For God so loved the world that He gave His only begotten son, that whatsoever believeth in Him should not perish, but have eternal life." (John 3:16) So I surrendered my life totally to Jesus Christ and I was saved from all sins. Praise the Lord!

Before I was saved and consecrated in the love of God, I understood love as a feeling between me and my girlfriend, Nelly. But Oh! God's love is different from earthly love because it is unconditional, with no strings attached. It is called AGAPE love.

The world today is striving for this love. No wonder the Bible speaks so clearly about this majestic theme. The value of God's love exceeds all other values in my life. May God help us all to experience His love in all its greatest degree and deepest dimension. Love is amazing, divine, supreme and vital. "Love is strong as death." (Song of Solomon 8:6) God loves you, "As the bridegroom rejoices over the bride, so shall God rejoice over you." (Isa. 62:5). Love will always find a way to express itself. God's love is redemptive. He gave His only son for us that He might redeem us from all iniquities. The true measure of God's love can be seen by a careful look of faith at Calvary's cross, where Jesus was crucified and voluntarily died for you and for me. God gave us His only son to be a living sacrifice for our sins, thus providing His greatest gift to us. I was born in sin with absolutely no saving grace of my own, nor meritorious works before God that I could cling to for my salvation. Therefore, my salvation is rooted in the love of God. For God's love in my life is better than gold that perishes. When I received Him in my heart, a fire of His love begun to grow in my heart, it went on till it became fire unspeakable and of great glory.

God Is Love

In every dimension you want to know God from love is the basic expression of His nature. Do not confuse His love with human love, which is always based upon self and selfish principals. Before I knew God's love I used to love those who loved me, I loved pleasures, my family and money. But when my inner eyes were suddenly opened to see and feel God's love flowing in my soul, I felt that divine love was all embracing love that went beyond the confines of my family and even my personal interests. "Here in his love, not that we loved God but he loves us, and sent His son to be the propitiation for our sins." (1 John 4:10)

My friend, may I introduce you to the everlasting lover of the world—Jesus Christ. He loves you very much, and today Jesus wants to deliver you from the bondage of bhang, marijuana, cocaine and heroin. He is able to set you free from alcohol, suicide, fornication, murder, rock and reggae music. The Bible says, "Ask, and it shall be given you; Seek, and you shall find; knock and it shall be opened unto you." (Luke 11:9) Call upon the name of Jesus now and experience His grace.

Dear friend, maybe you have tried everything the world has offered, without much success but now I urge you to come to Jesus. Jesus will conquer all your sins and make you a new creature. His name is love. I'm very glad for, "He brought me to the banqueting house, and His banner over me was love." (Song of Solomon 2:4) Jesus has invited you to come to the feasting house and celebrate together with Him for His victory on the cross. Come now, the decision is yours alone. God loves you so much and He has a wonderful plan for your life.

God's Love In My Life

By the grace of God I was and still am growing up spiritually day by day. The word of God revealed to me the love of God which passes all human understanding. I read in the Bible that love is kind, envies not, seeks not her own, it is not easily provoked, thinks of no evil and fails not. My soul was moved by God's awakening love which went deep into my being. I was led by God's redeeming love out in the open air, lifting up my voice like a trumpet to tell the world of their sin and the wonderful gift that awaits those who turn to God.

Surely charity begins at home. Every day in the evening, I would take my Bible and stand in a corner at my village to tell others about the love of God that forgives people their sins. I was totally involved in the fishing men business. No doubt they thought that I was crazy, because they could hear me speaking about Jesus, who is the savior of the world. And yet my past was bare before my folks. They couldn't accept the different attitude and sudden change in me.

Many people looked at me with suspicion as others clicked their tongues in disgust. I did not despise or fear opposition. I was not surprised when my friends failed me, because I knew that carnal minds do not grasp spiritual things. I maintained my ministry, which was to supply the whole village with the bread of life, which was covered, with the anointing of God.

To them it seemed strange, but to me it was an extraordinary ministry, to which Christ commissioned every believer. "Go ye therefore, and teach all nations, baptizing them in the name of the father, and of the son and the Holy Ghost." Matt. 28:19 I was doing God's will and I knew I had a great reward before God. I was never turned aside from the ministry, which the Lord urged me to do, I was serving my God with all my strength while the candle of God's love was still burning fast in my heart. I kept my calling free of personal affairs, politics or any other social indulgence. It was a divine call which satisfied and preoccupied my daily schedule leaving no room for other things.

Truly God's love must go forth if souls are to be saved. I was sowing the love seed in the hearts of men. The farmer sows the size of the field he expects to reap. I said, "Lord, I will sow the whole world with your word and expect you to give a good harvest." I knew God works with His word and in answer to prayers. I continued witnessing as the joy of the Lord began to fill me gradually till it became joy unspeakable and full of glory. I felt like bursting with praises of the Lord and my witness had great power.

The power of God fell on my village mates and there was a great awakening as the Lord's holy presence rested in the village. It was thrilling to see many coming to listen to the gospel and thereafter make anxious inquiries about the scriptures. Some began to read the gospel tracts I gave them.

Prayerfully and believingly, I witnessed of the gospel of love to the world. The power had come, because the word of God was alive in me, a fire burning in my bones, I was bold to minister the word with power. The word was piercing the hearts of men like a flaming sword. It had a great impact to the listeners. I preached to children, to the youth and in the open air and to a greater crowd. "He that wins souls is wise." (Prov. 11:30)

When I studied the ministries of the prophets and the apostles, I found a boldness, which was needed in my ministry. How urgently did I cling in faith and humility to God and expect Him to fill me with His power. It was evident that the Holy Spirit was working in the village, because they were becoming attentive to the word and asked a series of questions which only sin-troubled- souls ask. Even the village head, who was not attentive at first, came to listen to the word every day.

Many people began to attend our church and profess faith in Jesus. It was easy to hand over my life to God and take the gift of the Holy Spirit, but it was not easy to go in the village and tell people about the love of God. It was not easy to stand for God in the face of many trying, humiliating and almost heart breaking experiences. I did not know that I was to stand in trying circumstances, unjust criticisms, false accusations and frustrations. I stood firm in the lord because my faith worked with Love. (Gal 5:6).

But I thank God that he quickened my faith and I stood by His power. I trusted in God and not any human help. I laid every burden along with other failures and the fear of my future upon the LORD. God is faithful and His name is love. He saw me through the trying moments of witnessing, "From the day of John the Baptist until now the kingdom of God suffers violence, and the violent take it by force." (Math 11:12)

GODS SACRIFICIAL LOVE

ONE SUNDAY MORNING, at the church entrance, men and women stood quietly waiting to go in. They looked beautiful wearing their Sunday best. The sun was shining, spreading over the huge crowd; some were in red, others in pink and others with mixed colors. Women had made their hair and perfumed their bodies; this made the whole churchyard to look very beautiful. The cool morning breeze swayed the flowery plants that surrounded the church compound. I was excited this morning for some reason.

The senior pastor came with his wife and he greeted me warmly, then he told me I was to preach the word that Sunday, so I began to prepare for the sermon immediately. The church Pastor stood in front, turned to the brethren and said, "Come in brethren, and bring the drums." He was a tall country farmer, about forty years old, yet he was bowed at the shoulders by working many hours in the farm.

It was a lovely Sunday morning. The church was well-packed to capacity. The Pastor gave the opening hymn and as we sung we felt the atmosphere changing to one of pleasantry. At a distance the beats of the drums could be heard in one rhythm. Passersby stopped suddenly to listen to the interesting beats of the drums. People kept on coming, and an old man with scarred hands and bandaged legs came in and joined the praises.

After the singing, we all joined together in worshipping God, which took about thirty minutes. We sung one chorus and the deacon welcomed a few testimonies. We went on as the spirit led, it was certain that everybody wanted to say something about the wonderful love of God but unfortunately time ran out.

The Pastor stood to welcome me as the speaker. "You are welcome brother," he said. I stood and walked in the pulpit and in a moment everybody was silent, while I broke like tempest with the message of God's love. It was an inspiring message. The topic was "HOW GODS LOVE ARRESTED ME" I Read the word.

"His banner over me is love." (Song of Sol. 2:4) I lifted my voice like a trumpet as the words which were coming out of my mouth were full of Gods sacrificial love. The heavenly fire of God's love was burning in my spirit until it became fire unspeakable..

The brethren opened their mouths to shout with joy. Some banged the pews with excited shouts of "Amen." Everybody was smiling and the whole congregation was filled with bright faces. The sermon was simple; it was so powerful as many came to the Lord and promised to love God. Each one seemed captivated by heavenly love in their hearts. Heavenly grace was sinking slowly in their souls. We all felt a sweet sensation of the presence of the Most High God.

The message went on, while a volley of holy laughter shook the church hall. Both believers and unbelievers wanted to partake of the flowing blessings. Looking at my watch I noticed that my time was spent and I waved with a loud "Hallelujah," to which they all shouted, "Amen."

I left the pulpit to sit down and the Pastor took over, "Stand up brethren," he said. "The service is over." After the offerings he made an altar call. Many unbelievers came forward. You could see groups kneeling down before God for salvation. The pastor came to pray for them and this was the climax of the ceremony. He found the whole business extremely pleasant.

Sinners knelt down to receive what they had longed for. You could hear many confessing their sins in their own languages. Their sorrows vanished and something very redeeming came in their hearts. God's love was manifested in their lives for the first time. You could hear some praying and praising the Lord, "Stand up now!" the pastor requested, but a small group remained kneeling, praying and giving thanks to God for their salvation.

After the prayers everybody including the believers were deeply stricken by God's redeeming love. "Praise the Lord!" The pastor shouted and we shouted together "Amen." "Brethren," he said with an air of decision. "You have now received the tremendous experience of God's sacrificial love in your hearts. Let us sing one chorus." We all stood up in one voice, while the drums uttered an attentive growl. The whole congregation sang with ease as the spirit controlled. Each one felt a blessed sensation of God's sacrificial love. After the song he announced the end of the service; everybody left the church praising God for the revival. "He that wins souls is wise." (Prov. 11:30)

My friend, perhaps you did not attend this service, but you can receive this sacrificial love of God in your life today, just where you are, repent of your sins and God's sacrificial love will fill your heart now. This will be your revival. This divine love has no strings attached. It is unconditional love. Love without lust. This sacrificial love is very different from the lustful love of the world. It is agape love. You can read this detailed summary of my sermon below.

Love Seeketh Not Her Own.

Many people in the world profess to love God but they fail to separate themselves from, sins that the word of God reveals to us. The Bible says, "That which is born of God cannot sin because the seed of God is in him, that which sins is not of God, but belongs to

Satan who is the father and the founder of sin." (1 John 3:9) That's how we know the sons of God and the sons of the devil. A good relationship with God, to me, is based on His love. It is written, "Thou shalt love the Lord thy God with all thy heart and with all thy soul and with all thy mind." (Math. 22:37) After my salvation, God occupied the center of my thoughts, devotion, adoration and power. "The Lord preserveth all that love him but all the wicked will he destroy." (Psa. 145:20)

When Jesus came here on earth, the greatest thing He expressed to mankind and his chosen disciples was love. He said unto them, "These things I command you, that ye love one another." (John 14:34) To the disciples this commandment was new, for they had not yet grasped the real meaning of love. Love is the evidence of true practical discipleship. By love shall all men know that ye are my disciples. Love is the only power that joins man together and where this oneness exists, it is evident that the true image of God is manifested. Paul taught that, "Love seeketh not her own." (1 Cor. 13:5)

How many of us, when we have certain things, rights, benefits, or possession, refuse to strive at them and even refuse to keep some for yourself, but cheerfully give the others with great peace. The Bible says, "Great peace have they which love thy law and nothing shall offend them." Psa. 119:165)

When you falsely slander others, condemn, criticize, judge, or even murmur against anyone, no matter who he or she is or whatever he or she has done, it is enough proof that you have no love within yourself. Love thinks no evil, but covers all in silence and will not speak evil. Love works by being kind even under long continued suffering. When suffering in your life is maliciously caused by someone, love will always make you kind to that bad person and prevent you from taking revenge.

Love endureth all things. To endure is not simple; it is to pass through the fire or a very rough road on bare foot. How many of us can be able to pass through the fire or a very rough road on bare foot? How many of us can be able to pass through trying, hurtful, and false accusations on every side calmly as though they take no notice of the episode. Yet that is to endure.

I'm sure, if you will be really honest and measure yourselves by God's standards of genuine love, you shall see why you have failed to get the many things you have asked from God. You will find out whether your love is the genuine article shed abroad by the Holy Spirit in our heart, (Rom. 5:5). Jesus taught that, in John 14:23. A good prove that you love God is to keep His commandments. True love will cause our faith to bring quick answers for our prayers. Let us ask God now to give us the Holy Spirit to enable us to shed abroad His divine love in our hearts as the word promises.

Love Envies Not

Love envieth not, love does not desire position, honor, or favor or any blessing that another one has, but love will gladly see others enjoying their blessings and love would even help others to get more blessings rather than taking advantage. If we allow the love of God in our hearts, it won't be hard to love our brethren, our neighbors, the world, and even the great enemies. Love is the greatest power in this world and without God's love the world will grind to a halt and perish forever. God has called me to work for Him in love.

We are God's vessels, which he longs to fill with His divine love. When God fills our hearts with His love, there is no room for the works of the flesh. Every true Christian needs love from God. God makes us to increase and abound in His love. The real principal that makes us to know we have eternal life is love.

John taught, "Beloved in Christ, let us love one another; for love is of God and everyone that loveth is born of God; for God is love." (1 John 4:7). God is the source of all divine love. Paul, in Eph. 3:19, wants all saints to know deeply of this experience, the breadth, length, depth, and the height of love in Christ that passeth all knowledge, so that we all may be filled with the fullness of God. Many Christians today are not moved or motivated by the true love from God. I have experienced the love of God by the help of the Holy Spirit in my life and it is impossible to be separated from God.

I'm deeply convinced that even though the devil brings hardships, discouragement and persecution to me, God turns all this to strengthen me for His purpose and glory. "For all those who are called by God all things work for good." (Rom. 8:28)

Love Conquers

"I slept, but my heart moved and the voice of my beloved called, saying, 'Open for me my sweetie.' My beloved came into my heart. He is white and beautiful. His head and his hairs are white like wool. His eyes are like a flame of fire and His feet like fine brass, and His voice as the sound of many waters." (Rev. 1:14,15)

"He is my beloved. For many days, I used to kneel down unto the father of Jesus Christ and prayed that He might open my eyes and show me the beauties of heaven and I have been rejoicing in His glory. He has used many ways to express His love and He has also strengthened me with His spirit." Nay, in all these things we are more than conquerors through Him that loved us. For I am persuaded, that neither death, nor life, nor angels, nor principalities, nor powers, nor things present, nor any other creature, shall be able to separate us from the love of God, which is in Christ Jesus our Lord." (Rom. 37:39)

That's why I pray that the Lord may fill me with His love and soon I feel a warm benevolent feeling in my soul and so I praise the Lord and my soul utters a deep, "Amen."

I put the love of God in all walks of my life. "Beloved if God so loved us, we ought also to love one another. No man hath seen God at any time. If we love one another, God dwells in us, and his love is perfected in us." (1 John 4:11-12)

In my life now all works are accomplished by the regenerating power of God's love. I'm also given my share of joy, which makes Jesus Christ alive in me always. This love enables me to love all, even my enemies, while my hands help them in great compassion. Jesus shows me to love everybody.

He is the best example of love. He was nailed at the cross f or you and me but the only thing He said was, "Forgive them." Jesus is my savior and song, surely his banner over me is love. Through love the Lord has blessed me in many ways. "He raised up the poor out of the dust and beggars from the dunghill, to set them among princess, and to make them inherit the throne of glory: For the pillars of the earth are the Lord's and he hath set the world upon them." (1 Sam. 2:8)

His Banner Over Me Is Love

Suddenly He saved me.

One who was affected by sins and fears,

A sinner born to die in hell forever In love He spoke to my heart His banner over me is love.

Surely His name is love, who died for me

One who was lost forever

But tasted His glorious love and power By faith I saw Him face to face His banner over me is love.

Yes! He loved me unconditionally

Jesus the sinners' friend

He who overcame death for you and me I will love Him to the end for His banner over me is love.

Weak and poor

Hell, earth and sin overcame me

But by the blood of Jesus I'm free Jesus is above my joy and His banner over me is love.

He is my sweetie, in heaven

How wonderful is He, my beloved

He is in the inner chambers of my heart He is my master, deeply in love His banner over me is love. The sermon ends.

• • • •

CHAPTER NINE

FREE FROM FALSE HOPES

I SAT BESIDE THE FIREPLACE opposite my family, deeply considering my spiritual condition in the sight of God. I was both relaxed and excited by a wonderful and thrilling revelation of the scriptures that came to my mind.

I looked at my Bible again. What a lovely piece of truth! I thought of the days of my past life in Jesus. I felt proud, too, because in every page I could find everything to satisfy my longing and without doubt I believed that the Bible was the Word of God, full of wonderful promises, which were so appealing to me. My heart throbbed faster as I remembered the night when Jesus peered into my soul and made me a completely new person. I shall never forget the feeling in me. I was overwhelmed by emotions as the past memories came to my mind and I thought, I am free from false hopes!

Without Jesus, my life had no meaning. It was miserable, empty, confused and frustrated. I had no hope. But now, with Jesus at the center of it, there is an inner strength, peace, a deep satisfaction and unfading joy. By receiving Jesus Christ as my personal Savior, I was born again. It required no effort of mine that I might obtain this spiritual blessing, but as I believed so it happened. Praise His wonderful name, Jesus!

"I prevented the dawning of the morning, and cried. I hope in thy word." (Psa. 119:147) By faith, I was given power to become a Son of God who was very far from religious observations and nurtured false hopes, which are increasing in the world today. And yet many blinded people are resting their hopes upon dead doctrines. Surely so much error and confusion exists among many as to where the spiritual blessings can be found. Let me say that, even though beautiful and impressive religious cathedrals are constructed, men and women are still longing for the blessing which is promised by the true word of God.

In the Bible we read, "Remember the word unto thy servant, upon which thou hast caused me to hope." (Psa. 119:49) You may say, "I read the Bible daily in my life." Does reading the Bible daily make you a Christian? No! Jesus said, "Verily, verily, I say unto thee, except a man be born again, he cannot see the kingdom of God." (John 3:3) Are you a born again believer in Jesus Christ? Are your sins forgiven through His cleansing blood? If you have inward witness of the spirit in the word of salvation, you can never be a member of Christ's church on earth.

A member of the divine family which includes holy angels and all blood washed saints from every nation and every age. So don't assume that attending religious services or reading the Bible makes you a Christian. No! Unless the power of the living God does something in you, you will perish in hell.

Many people today lay their hope of salvation on such things as sacraments, pilgrimages, burning candles, or priests, etc. But I always ask, "Did Jesus teach any such doctrine of dead traditions?" Surely No! For there is no sect, bishop, priest, ordinance or sacrament on earth that can save your sinful life or give you inward peace, love and joy. You may blindly join in the best sect in the world be most faithful to its doctrines, and yet be lost in hell forever, so what is the use?

I have the witness of God's power in my life for I am a born-again believer, and I know by faith that my name is written in the book of life. I also have received the infilling of the Holy Spirit and do speak in tongues. His spirit has also forged a bond between Jesus and His body who are the holy blood washed saints worldwide. I also fellowship with brethren, which means to share the word of God with other believers in a local assembly. For the word of God says, "Not forsaking the assembling of ourselves together, as the manner of some is; but exhorting one another and so much more, as ye see the day approaching." (Heb. 10:25)

I did not let my relatives push me into their own religion and I was not impressed by their nice ministers or their big cathedrals. But I trusted on the Lord Jesus Christ who gave a clear pattern of worship in the book of Acts. It is obvious that by much prayer and Bible study, I understood God's will. God is ever faithful if our eyes of faith are fixed on Him only. He works miracles. By faith he led Moses and the people of God. He gave them a clear pattern of worship. He said, "Who serve unto the example and shadow of heavenly things, as Moses was admonished of God when he was about to make the tabernacle: for, see, saith he, that thou make all things according to the pattern showed to thee in the mount." (Heb.8:5)

The building you worship in, whether it be at home, a hall, a big cathedral, has no spiritual significance whatsoever. Read the Bible well and you find that it is the worshippers who are the church and not the building. Therefore, you must not allow any superstitious awe of buildings or sect dignitary or Hollywood style liturgy to dominate your thinking or make you decide your choice of fellowship. Remember that, "Howbeit the Most High dwelleth not in the temples made with hands, as saith the prophet." (Act 7:48)

You had better receive Jesus as your savior now by obeying God's word and straight away you promise to commit yourself to obedience to God's word in every department of your life, and you will be a son of God. As a disciple of Jesus Christ, I do not lead myself. I will never allow any sect dignitary to assume God's authority. He is my Lord and in Him will I give account without the false advocacy of a priest or minister. When I finally settled in my fellowship, I was able to say before them that, "God has led me into this fellowship."

I was separated from this sinful world and it's ways and it's companionship. I could no longer attend movies or discos. For I was a new creature. God forbids this in His word, "Therefore if any man be in Christ he is a new creature: Old things are passed away; behold, all things have become new." (2 Cor. 5:17) Therefore, I have to obey the word. In my fellowship with other believers, God was present in the Holy Spirit and I recognized His presence when the word quickened my spirit and stimulated my faith and drew out a strong desire to tell others of this wonderful experience.

After my salvation, my old habits changed and I became an avid reader of Christian books by anointed men of God. I received power and I grew in the word of faith. Therefore, I had a consuming desire to preach the gospel and finally I have surrendered my life to the ministry.

So if you are not born again, you cannot be a member of the holy spiritual church that Jesus founded. The word "church" translated from the Greek, simply means a called out gathering of born-again believers. Those people who have separated themselves from the world to serve God through Jesus, His son. The church is not a building as you tend to think. It is a sure sign that you are really born-by the power of the spirit of God, when your soul thirsts for the truth and your heart is drawn to other believers with a desire to learn more of Jesus Christ from His word.

You must not want to be saved, unless you feel that you are lost in sin, nor would you plead to be rescued, unless you were drowning. You would never call for a doctor unless you are sick and then you would never call for Jesus to save you unless you fell that you are a lost sinner. The Bible says, "For whosoever shall call upon the name of the Lord shall be saved." (Rom. 10:13)

Beware of any hope that is not drawn from the Bible. It is a false hope. Jesus alone is the sure foundation of a Good Hope. He is the tried stone "Wherefore also it is contained in the Scriptures, behold I lay in Zion a chief cornerstone, elect precious: and he that believeth on him shall not be confounded." (1 Peter 2:6)

Lord Thou Art My Hope

Lord I do trust in thee from my youth

Upon thee I have learned after the new birth Thou art thee who saved me from hell Lord thou art my hope.

I have been a laughing stock to my friends

But Lord thou art my strong refuge

My mouth is filled with thy praise

And thy glory all the day long Do not cast me off from the Lord thou art my hope.

Lord make haste to help me

Let them fail who seek my life

Rescue me, O Lord from the wicked generation

Be quick to deliver me

For in thee Lord do I take refuge Lord thou art my hope.

Thou art my hope and my salvation

While my enemies are against me

Let them be confused who seek my life

And I will hope thee continually And praise thee more and more Lord thou art my hope.

Lord thou has crushed the oppressor

And thou has given me eternal life

My lips will shout for joy and sing praises

Dear Lord thou art good to me May thy Name be praised forever for Lord thou art my Hope.

· · · ·

CHAPTER TEN

HIGHER LIFE IN JESUS

FOR MANY YEARS I HAVE known that I received the gift of eternal life when I received Jesus Christ as my personal savior. God became real the moment I repented my sins to Him. The power of the living and merciful God came into my heart and I was now stepping in the divine sphere in relationship with God as a son. Praise the Lord!

Many people confuse eternal life with external existence, but there is a vast difference between the two. Many verses of scripture prove that every human being will have eternal existence after death, but all will not have eternal life, which is the gift of God. Some will be in everlasting punishment and some into eternal life, which is received by faith.

Speaking of eternal life, Jesus said, "My sheep hear my voice, and I know them, and they follow me." (John 10:27) Note that as the sheep hears and follows eternal life is given. If the sheep stops hearing and following, then that life begins to be withheld, and soon the sheep dies eternally. We all need to understand that eternal life is so called because it is the gift of God alone. Speaking of eternal life, David said, "Thou wilt show me the path of life, in thy presence is fullness of joy, at thy right hand there are pleasures for evermore." (Psalm 16:11) "If you receive eternal life you will also have righteous peace and joy in the Holy Ghost." (Rom. 14:17)

If you have not received this joy now, how will you have it in the presence of Christ at the day of judgment? Eternal life is the out-breathed life of God through Jesus Christ. To receive eternal life is to receive His imparted nature and so we become consequently like God – Hallelujah.

"For as the father hath life in Himself, so hath he given to the son to have life in himself." (John 5:25) That truth is plain. "He that hath the son hath life, and he that hath not the son of God hath not life." (1 John 5:12) If we seek a pearl we must find an oyster, for the oyster provides the pearl. So if you want eternal life, you must find Christ experientially, for eternal life is in Him. He is the God- appointed fountain of life, available to all who thirst for it, to all who have recognized that they are dead in trespasses and in sins. Jesus a fountain of living water, and by drinking from this foundation you is will have life eternal.

When the starving Jews came to pharaoh for bread he said, "Go unto Joseph, what he saith to you do," (Gen. 41:55) because pharaoh had given the responsibility of sharing the bread to Joseph. So now, to all those who are starving for eternal life and want to seek pardon for sins, the Holy Father says, "This is my beloved son ... hear Him." And the mother of Jesus said, "Whatsoever he saith unto you, do it." (John 2:5)

Standing among a crowd of religious but spiritually dissatisfied people, Jesus cried, "If any man thirst, let him come unto me, and drink. (John 7:37) Therefore indicating that ETERNAL LIFE is received by drinking in faith. Even you, can receive ETERNAL LIFE now. John, in the book of Revelation, saw the life of God pouring forth in a river clear as crystal, proceeding out of the throne of God and the lamp. From this river all who are thirsty are invited to drink. (Rev. 22:17) Only those who find this world a dry and thirsty land are invited to come to Christ to drink. There is a secret of being a man after God's own heart like David who said: "O God, thou art my God, early will I seek thee, my soul thirsts for thee, my flesh longs for thee in a dry thirsty land where no water is." (Psalm 63:1)

The depth of our spiritual life can be assessed by the thirst we have for the things of God which seems to satisfy many Christians today. The God of love is the reservoir of eternal life and through Jesus the Savior, the Floodgates are wide open in mercy to any repentant sinner. Jesus says to you now, "If any one thirst let him come unto me, and drink." (John 7:37)

All that God asks is that His people be willing to receive His great mercy and grace. What is considered a blessed experience is to be a receiver and praise rather than a legalistic doer of the good deeds. To be an earthen vessel before the Lord into which Jesus continually pours heavenly treasures and blessings of love, peace, joy and power. The flood of His glory is pouring into souls in awakening words and songs of praise.

This is expressible for He fills the whole being with His Holy redeeming passion and the unspeakable gift of God's love. This is the land of God's rest where one can experience His love and learn to draw nearer His nature and power. This is salvation in full. This is how we learn by simple faith to receive what God has promised in His word. Ask yourself why you haven't received this higher life in Jesus.

Sitting before God's presence, I read in the Bible about many people who had the offer of eternal life and by disobeying God they lost their lives. An example of them being Judas Iscariot who committed spiritual suicide by sinning when he betrayed the Son of God. (Acts 1:25) I learnt that the moment those Holy ones disobeyed God in stepping out of their divine given sphere, they lost their titles as sons of God. They were cut off from the fountain of eternal life. Cut off from the higher life of peace, joy and freedom in Jesus Christ. They will never recover what they lost because they died and their sins are before God's throne.

Our God is Holy so He also wants us to be Holy. Even the Angels around His throne are Holy because of His imparted life which makes them holy and in one mind and heart with himself. The secret of becoming holy is therefore obviously found in Jesus Christ. Jesus Christ's indwelling is the answer to every human need and He accomplishes in us what our diligent faith holds onto.

Whether it be holiness, pure heart, endowment with power, divine healing or any other blessings promised by the word. We only receive what we hunger after and get hold of it by faith. All these blessings are entered into our hearts by an act of faith. Many lose this genuine spiritual experience because they do not understand the law of faith.

By faith you can receive any of these blessings, but—first of all—receive eternal life. God loves you. Our God is merciful and gracious, long-suffering and abounding in goodness and truth." (Ex. 34:6) You must promise to fulfill His commandment. "Because it is written, Be ye holy for I am holy." (1 Peter 11:16) Salvation in its completeness is the gift of God received through faith.

My personal appeal is; Are you thirsty? A vessel is set before you full of living water, but until you raise that vessel to your lips and receive the water into your stomach you will remain thirsty. You must drink or perish. So you must take by faith the free pardon Jesus offers you through His own blood.

CHAPTER ELEVEN

MY FAITH WORKS

WHAT IS FAITH? "FAITH is the substance of things hoped for, the evidence of things not seen," (Heb. 11:1) So then faith comes by hearing the word. After hearing the word it goes down into your dry soul and creates hope in you. By faith, God wants you to receive first the gift of salvation, healing, righteousness, peace and the power of the Holy Spirit.

Jesus taught, "Therefore I say unto you, what things, so ever ye desire, when ye pray, believe that ye receive them, and ye shall have them." (Mark 11:24) It is plain from the Bible that believing is receiving from God. Christians, have you ever received any of these blessings promised by God in His Word? Believe now and receive salvation in Jesus Christ. It is yours for the asking!

Many people have an intellectual faith. The faith of knowing that there is Jesus the Savior of all, but not a personal Savior in their soul. The faith of religion which believes Jesus is the LORD and King of our lives. The faith of praying, "LORD give us your Holy Spirit," but not in my soul. This is a universal (general) kind of faith. But a closer relationship between an individual and God is necessary.

This way you will know God in a personal way and become your closest friend. There are two types of faith: intellectual faith and faith that is born by the word. "So then faith cometh by hearing, and hearing by the word of God." (Rom. 10:17) The latter sort of faith has works and these works are the fruits of God, which qualifies it as inspired faith. The former type of faith, intellectual faith, is the idea of having the knowledge of God in the mind but not in the heart. This sort of faith does not please God; it is vain and does not receive anything from God. It is a dead faith.

Many Christians today profess that they love Jesus and yet they are empty of this inward blessing from Him. They worship Jesus as an idol and not as a living personality. Thousands are trying to persuade themselves that by reading some verses in the Bible about the life of Jesus and becoming emotional they have a good faith in Him. Yet they don't receive benefits from their faith. These are the present false teachers and blind leaders. They profess what they have not received. From such idolaters, I keep myself at a clear distance.

So you think you are as Christian because you believe that there is God, Jesus and the Holy Spirit. The demons also believe that and tremble. Believing in God without receiving His blessings and growing in the knowledge is useless. This kind of faith is a demon-inspired faith. It has no works. (James 2:17-18)

"But wilt thou know, O vain man, that faith without works is dead." (James 2:20) Anyone who claims that he believes in God, and has not received blessings such as new birth in the spirit, is not yet converted and has everything to learn. He is like stuffed beasts in Nairobi Museum. Dead beasts which are cold and motionless. Lifeless shells before God. Where there is life there is will and feeling of inward life. Any faith that does not profess power from above and is not rooted inwardly is not from God. God is alive and His life is power.

So the kingdom of God is not the knowledge of Him in your brain but the power in your heart and in your life. "For the kingdom of God is not in word, but in power." (1 Cor. 4:20) So let no man deceive you with vain words. "Little children, let no man deceive you: he that doeth righteousness is righteous, even as He is righteous. He that commiteth sin is of the devil, for the devil sinneth from the beginning." (1 John 3:7,8) Any faith that does not change you and make you just, honest, truthful, sober, meek, kind and righteous in all relationships is not from God.

Demons know God better than any human being in the world, for they were in God's presence long before the world was created and, by disobeying God, they were cast out of His presence eternally. There is no hope for them. It is the power of demons in the minds and hearts of men that filled the world with violence and wickedness in Noah's days which brought about their destruction by water. It can be compared with the evil and hypocritical minds of the scribes and Pharisees which led to the death of our Savior.

The same hypocrites are active in the churches and in our so-called enlightened generation. So if you want to be delivered from evil powers, call unto the name of Jesus Christ. "For whosoever shall call upon the name of the Lord shall be saved." (Rom. 10:13) If you have not yet received the gifts of God in your Christian life, I urge you to believe the Lord for the same so as to function fully in the Church of Christ.

Faith that does not exercise a sanctifying influence in your heart, in your conduct and your conversation, is a demon-inspired faith. It is a show off of your religion. Anyone with a Godly faith is careful about the world and the wiles of the devil. But anyone who allows habitual sins to creep in is rotten in his heart. He may talk of his faith as much as he pleases, but he is a stumbling block to the world and he is a shame to born-again Christians. The reason why the Bible says, "In all labor there is profit, but the talk of the lips tendeth only to penury." (Pro. 14:23)

In these last days there are many who claim that they have received the kingdom of God, but their actions reveal that they do not know God. "They profess that they know God but in works they deny Him, being abominable, and disobedient, and unto good work reprobate." (Titus 1:6) We have many of these examples in every religion, seeing them in the pews on Sunday one would say, "Hey these are true Christians," and yet they are involved in all worldliness, e.g.: drunkenness.

The partaking of sacraments is no foundation of good faith. You may eat it every Sunday and even be sprinkled with holy water on your head and yet know nothing of the water of life in experience. Jesus said about drinking the living water that He alone is the source of living water, (John 4:14-15)

Many people commit this common sin today. The sin of abandoning Jesus Christ the living water and venturing in vain to find living water elsewhere. In the early days the people of Israel had done these two evils, "For my people have hewed them out cisterns, broken cisterns that can hold no water." (Jer. 2:13) God is speaking to your conscience right now. It is a moment of great possibility and also a moment of great danger. Disobedience will lead you into everlasting destruction. The decision is yours alone.

But I urge you to "Choose Life." If you believe in God, then you must accept that you are as guilty as hell. If you are honest with your own heart you know that you need a savior to save you from your sins. Will you take a step of faith right now and acknowledge your helplessness? Jesus is faithful. He will lead you into greener pastures beside still waters. Ask Him to save you today. Thank God for opening your eyes before it is too late, like the rich man in Luke 16:23.

The merciful God who has showed you your lost condition in your sins, has done so that He might show you the savior, whom He has provided for you. It is plain from the scriptures that anyone who believes receives. Have you ever received the blessing of salvation from God? If you will not receive this gift your judgment will be the same with the trembling demons. Jesus will say to you: "Depart from me, ye cursed into everlasting fire prepared for the devil and his angels." (Matt. 25:41)

Let me share with you my personal testimony, "If Jesus did not die for my sins, I would not have a hope of escaping punishment for my sins." But now I thank the Lord God that Jesus died for me. Glory to God for His mercy! If you don't receive Christ now you will answer for your own sins with terrible consequences. You are now hearing God's voice commanding you to turn from the pleasures and receive Jesus as your personal savior ... what is your ANSWER?

Answering for your sins on the judgment day will be serious enough. But not nearly so serious as answering for rejecting God who sent Jesus as our Savior. Remember Jesus is your judge. Please believe in Him now. Believing what God promised is receiving from Him. Why don't you do so and see? God is real to me and MY FAITH WORKS.

CHAPTER TWELVE

BELIEVING IS RECEIVING

ARE YOU TERMINALLY ill? Are you a drunkard or an Aids victim, a drug addict, a sex pervert, a slave of Satan in any way? If you are a sinner, the future can look grey and miserable. Eternity is a terrifying word to think of when one feels he is standing on its brink.

Do you know that God in His infinite love has permitted you to come to this extremity that he might make Himself known to you? It is only when human beings get into hopeless situations that they are open to listen to God's voice.

From my own experience I can assure you that out of your present distress our God can bring you the greatest blessing you have ever known. Please believe this. The Bible says, "And all things whatsoever ye shall ask in prayer, believing ye shall receive." (Matt. 21:22) Jesus invites you to ask for your salvation and your healing now.

If you could only believe, His hand is stretched out to touch you at this very moment. All you need to do is to receive Him by faith. He cannot work without your cooperation. He cannot give the gift of salvation until you put your faith into action.

This is what the scripture means: "But without faith it is impossible to please Him." (Heb. 11:6) When in prayer, believe that God has heard your prayer the first time you pray, because God does not need to be coaxed to answer prayers. It is important that you understand this, otherwise, you will pray in vain repetitions and get nothing in the end. God hears prayers the first time you pray in earnest. Jesus is saying to you now: "Who forgiveth all thine iniquities who healeth all thy diseases." (Psalm 103:3)

Jesus expects you to respond in faith saying, "Thank you Lord I take you at your word and believe that you have forgiven me now." It is not praying that makes you obtain, but believing is receiving. Hear what Jesus said before raising a man from the dead, "Said I not unto thee, that if thou wouldest believe thou shouldest see the glory of God." (John 11:40) Many people today like hearing about God, but they do not want to believe in Him; hence, they can't see the glory of God. (Job 42:5)

Believing must always come before seeing or feeling, so do not be surprised, if you feel a little change after receiving salvation or healing. Jesus comes in very softly; it is almost certain that Satan tries to resist the fullness of salvation or healing in order to try your faith. Never let down God's promises when you pray. Never doubt that God has saved you or healed you when you believed. Keep on thanking and praising Jesus, as He is still working in your life. He will not fail you no matter how helpless your case is. Be content to praise and to stand on God's words.

We have a good instance of this in the cleansing of the lepers. Having accepted Jesus word, "They walked on in trust and as they went they were cleansed." (Luke 17:14) Immediately they believed the healing process started and it became fully manifested in their bodies. We have a similar instance in John 4:50, where the healing power of Christ was immediately set in motion when the nobleman accepted His word in faith.

If you believe His saving power is working in you, then confess your faith to someone as commanded by God in Romans 10:9-10. Simply say "Jesus Christ is saving me now," and point to the word as a proof. Others may believe too. There is nothing that is more faith-strengthening than a bold confession of your mouth. Read II Corinthians 4:13. We believe and speak what we believe.

What is my scriptural authority for expecting God to answer my prayers at the first time? It is found in Mark 11:24. "What things soever you ask, when you pray, believe you receive and ye shall have them." Note that the Lord did not say that I was to receive in future, but it said "Believe you receive." This simply means that whatever need you have, God will meet it at this minute, if you believe you receive. Believing is the condition of receiving.

When I learnt to exercise this faith I have never remained the same. It is like plugging into divine power while praises keep the power flowing. Each burden I have and each need I have, I normally commit it to God in definite faith, whether it be healing, sanctification, power for service or deliverance from demon bondage.

I believe God gives and I am freed from the burden and free from the miserable bondage of repetitive praying, that so wearies the soul and destroys faith. Suppose it takes time to obtain the blessings I keep on praising God for, reminding my heart of my faith transaction and God's faithfulness. (Rom. 4:18-25) When I learnt this way of praising, then I knew a new way of living and saw quicker answers to my prayers, especially in my own life in matters of sanctification and spiritual power.

Praise performs wonders, which somehow prayers cannot. When I thank God, even if I'm in severe tests of faith, I find the spirit of God flooding my soul in a wonderful way. Let me tell you that it is not easy to praise God when in pain or weakness or when brokenhearted. It is not easy to praise God when everything seems opposite. But I can assure you from my own experience that praise is the sure way of victory. (Read Acts 16:25-26; 2nd Chron. 20:20).

No matter how hopeless the situation, no matter how hard-hearted is the person we are praying for, the praise of faith works wonders. Praise hooks the fish, praise lands it on shore. What a difference it makes in my life when I wake up in the morning with thanks and praise on my lips for the wonders God did for me the previous day and for the marvelous things He is going to do today, and every day, till I see His face.

A life filled with such praise is a holy, God pleasing life. The law of faith applies to the vilest sinner who honestly wants to seek God. Apart from this faith there is no one who will ever receive pardon nor experience the saving power of Jesus Christ. Faith is the key to every blessing. Christians who are enjoying secret sins or who hold grudges need not offer this prayer of faith. God does not hear hypocrites unless they repent, and say now, "Behold Jesus Christ is my salvation, I will trust and not be afraid for the Lord Jehovah is my strength and song. He also became my salvation." (Isa. 12:2) He is your savior when you so claim Him. It is not a question of feeling saved or healed. It is a question of taking God at His word.

It cannot be emphasized enough that in any faith transaction we must absolutely disregard our feelings. What we feel and what we see are very often Satan's weapons to make us disbelieve God's word. What God says is fact to faith. (Read Heb. 11:1, II Cor. 4:18) We walk by faith and not by sight.

What is your need at this moment? Jesus is speaking to you now, saying have faith in God (Mark 11:22), and then speak to your mountain. (Mark 11:23) Command your mountain to leave in Jesus name! Jesus Christ can break every sin and disease that

Satan has brought to you, the Lord is saying, "I am the Lord that healeth thee." (Exodus 15:26)

Why not believe He is SPEAKING TO YOU and promising to deliver you. Take by faith His saving and healing power. Say to Him now, "Jesus will you come into my life in saving power and completely deliver me from evil." My friend, if you refuse Jesus Christ, what other hope have you? Believe now and receive now. (Matt. 21:22) Speak to your problem and command it to leave in Jesus Name. God bless you.

CHAPTER THIRTEEN

WHAT MUST I DO TO BE SAVED?

ONE DAY, THERE WAS a man named Saul in the land of Israel. He claimed to be a Christian, who exercised his faith in persecuting and threatening the followers of Jesus Christ. Saul had no idea that God lived in the hearts of His saints through Jesus Christ. Suddenly when he was on the way to Damascus to persecute the followers of Jesus Christ, he fell on the ground and heard a voice saying unto him, "Saul why persecuteth thou me?" He was surprised and he began trembling in fear. He asked, "Who art thou, Lord?" And the Lord answered him, "I'm Jesus whom thou persecutes." (Acts 9:3-5)

Saul lay down helplessly before a mighty God, who He was persecuting without knowing. He cried for salvation and he was saved. He was transformed by the power of Jesus Christ, out of being a persecutor into a wonderful preacher of the gospel of Jesus Christ. "And straight away he preached Christ in the synagogues, that he is the Son of God." (Acts 9:20)

My friend, perhaps you call yourself a Christian, but you do not know God through His Son Jesus Christ, personally. You might be a Christian by your lips but your actions reveal that you are a sinner like Saul. You need salvation, which comes from Jesus Christ only.

Now God wants to save and transform you into a new creature that the power of God will be in you forever. Suddenly as it happened to Saul, it can happen to you, if only you believe that there is a powerful God who lives and who knows your hidden actions. God knows your name and all your sins; you cannot deceive God. When Saul was living in sin and persecuting the followers of Jesus Christ, he thought in his heart that he was serving God. But God saw these evil actions and knew that Saul was in darkness. So by the power of the living God, Saul saw a great light in his life. He was delivered from religious practices. He was saved and later he received the Holy Spirit. (Acts 9:17)

After he was filled with the Holy Spirit, He became a powerful preacher of the gospel. He preached about the power of God that transformed him, he said that he knew God, Jesus and the Holy Spirit. He preached with the power of the Holy Spirit; he went about destroying false hopes and he assured people that God does not live in the temples made with hands. (Acts 17:24)

Many people confess that they love God and are serving Him, but they do not know Him in experience. They are living in sin, just like Saul. Good feelings in your heart, without Jesus, do not make you a Christian. Some people say with their lips that they are Christians, but when life becomes windy and stormy they fall helplessly. Every true Christian must be tested to prove that they know the God whom they believeth and are properly saved. You may belong to the best sect or a cult and miss the joy of serving the living son of God, Jesus Christ.

Today in our religions thousands of people think that by going to church every Sunday to pray and give offerings and alms to the poor that they are saved. In the Bible, there was a man in Caesarea called Cornelius, a centurion of the band called the Italian band. He was a devout man, and one that feared God with his entire house, which gave much alms to the people, and he prayed to God always. He was a good soldier who feared God, but all his good works did not save him until God sent an angel to him and told him to call Peter who was a minister of the gospel. When Peter came at the home of this man and ministered the gospel of life to him, his house and his friends they were all saved and were filled with the Holy Spirit and later they were baptized. (Acts 10)

God loves you very much; He does not care about your rank, your tribe or the color of your skin. God is not a respecter of persons, but "in every nation that feareth Him, and worketh righteousness, He dwelleth in their midst. (Acts 10:34-35) Note the word 'righteousness'. There is no salvation outside Jesus Christ. You cannot be righteous before God without accepting Jesus into your heart. Jesus was made sin for us and we are the righteousness of God. (II Cor. 5:21)

When I received Jesus Christ in my heart, I became righteous before God. I have a right stand before my creator. He lives in my heart and works in my life. I'm always ready to explain to anyone how I found eternal life. When your faith in Christ is sound, you must be able to show it clearly in your life and actions. Great knowledge without salvation is useless.

A man may have three degrees in divinity and even teach many theological colleges yet, without Jesus, he will be lost in hell forever. An old village woman like my grandmother may be unable to read and even have a weak understanding of God's requirement for salvation but, by her simple faith in Jesus Christ, she can be saved. Many people waste their time studying the Bible and yet they reject Jesus Christ as their savior.

Once I approached a lady in our church and talked to her about salvation. She thought that she was a Christian because she was very kind. She liked attending church every Sunday and she was in the church choir. She kept herself very smart with well-made hair, with complimentary features. She was generous and had a loving heart. Though she was active in the things of God, I saw that she was struggling to reach heaven on her own, by her good works.

She looked at me with an ironical expression, sat down briskly and asked me, "What must I do to be saved?" I smiled at her and said "Sister, to be saved is to repent all your sins and receive Jesus Christ as your personal savior." She was glad to learn this bare truth. I continued. "Sister, this is your chance to be saved."

She paused, as the gospel was sinking deep in her heart. With a wiser reflection and a well-timed approach, I inquired softly, "It seems bogus to you, but Jesus Christ is the only way to life." She was a good lady but without the gospel. I told her to abandon her own will and imaginations. But she was too innocent to believe the gospel, because she believed that her works were fair. She felt something very real at that moment, but she resisted the calling.

"Sister!" I called, "Jesus loves you; he died on the cross and the blood He shed was for the remission of your sins." I told her to forsake all sins and forget any boyfriend in her life. She began to feel her sinfulness, she felt guilty. But before she received Jesus Christ, she thought about her easy life and promised to be saved later.

After some days she began attending our meetings. She used to sing with us joyfully. One day she knelt before the brethren and began to cry for salvation. She was ushered into the kingdom as she received Jesus Christ as her personal savior. We all danced with joy and welcomed her to testify. She now enjoyed what she had been longing for and she had a very moving and interesting testimony. After some days, she was filled with the Holy Ghost and became a bold witness of Christ, praise the Lord. God is real to all those who seek Him by faith.

With a smile she became used to confessing how she felt a great change in her life, and we saw the change in her life. She would talk about her goodness, but she knew nothing about the grace of

God. She became crazy before her village friends because she was ready to tell anybody about her newfound faith, with a deep feeling within she could shout, "Jesus is my savior."

Today she is a wonderful gospel singer in our church and a effectual soul winner. She is now married to a young man in our church and they are both singers.

You might be like this good lady who could be lost because of believing in her own works. Why are you afraid to ask, like this lady, "What must I do to be saved?" Believe in Jesus Christ and thou shall be saved. (Acts 1:23) God loves you so much.

CHAPTER FOURTEEN

WHERE ARE YOU HEADING TO?

YES! WE LIVE IN A MOST dangerous day; a day when lawlessness, immorality, inflation and corruption are running swiftly. When every kind of evil is displayed in every nation so plainly. Crime and violence is increasing, and our prisons are overflowing with condemned criminals and suspects.

Earthquakes and rumors of wars are the present news in the medias, while the falling apart of the world's economy is the talk of the day. The world is tearing asunder and millions are sitting in the shadow of death, not knowing which way to turn for help.

On the other hand, reports of the rapid spreading disease, HIV/Aids, is increasing in every nation on earth. Now from every corner of the world there is fear and collision. No wonder that destruction is ahead of us, surely every one may be excused to ask, "Oh dear, what is the world coming to?" We are a part of a worried and anxious generation, which is almost at the brink of death. This is a dying world full of incurable diseases, famine and corruption, symptoms of unholiness that have prevailed since the fall of Adam.

Soon or later, everyone is sensing that something terrible is about to happen. This world is tearing at the human history. Now and then people are turning to their Bibles to see what it says about the end of the world. But may I assure you, that the Bible does not say too much about that day but the little it says is crucial. There are signs to show us clearly that Jesus is coming soon.

Despite the great work of man in scientific advancement, the world is still in the bondage of sin, suffering and shameful. The need of salvation is great, because man is still a slave of Satan, while the virus of sin's poison is deep in his senses and conscience. Satan is leading man to the slaughter house (hell) making him to dance the death dance, which Satan is piping. Can you see that you are helpless, your condition is terrible, you are trapped, bound foot and hands. You are a prisoner, doomed and externally lost forever. Sin is a heavy burden in your life that you would not dare to take the risk, if only you knew the dangers.

There is work to be done in your life. Work that will challenge every sin in your life. Work that will remove every bad thought in your mind and every evil motive in your soul. It is definitely the work of God and the labor of Jesus Christ and the engagement of the Holy Spirit. I'm sure that you will find that it is a glorious work of the cross; even though men despise it, it is the only power out of which man's soul can derive peace. Many people today have rejected God while living in this world, but pretend to find help when dying or when in great pain or in trouble.

I have frequently heard people saying that they felt quite ready to go to heaven when they are at the point of death; they say that they desired nothing in this world, and yet these people are ignorant of the gospel of Christ and know nothing of a single truth. Unless they repent their sins before thy die, thy will be dashed straight in hell.

There is no scrap of solid hope here on earth, rather than Jesus Christ. I believe that everybody on earth, even the philosopher, the scientist, the doctor, and the theologian must each be constant by seeking living water in Jesus Christ. It is not enough to have good feelings in your soul and think that you will go to heaven after death and yet you have no faith in Jesus Christ, that's wishful thinking, which will never materialize.

God loves you very much. He looks at your sinful life and longs to save you from death. He is ready to fill you with His divine power through His Son Jesus Christ. God is not a respecter of persons; He loves you just as you are. I know many people who have had wonderful experiences of the new birth by the power of God; some have seen visions of the Lord appearing unto them at night. Believe the Lord to use you for he uses ordinary people like you and I.

Ignorant people say that there are many ways to heaven. But the Bible talks of two ways—only one of which leads to heaven. You have a good chance to choose which way to follow now. There is the narrow way and the wide way. The wide way is found by many people today, because it is the way of destruction.

The narrow way is found by very few, because it is the way of life eternal. Jesus is the way and you cannot ignore Him for there is no other way that leads to God. Jesus is not a signboard, He is the way, enter ye in at the gate. "For wide is the gate and broad is the way, that leadeth to destruction, and many are they which go there at: Because straight is the gate, and narrow is the way which leadeth unto life and few are they that find it." (Math. 7:13-14)

"There is a way which seemeth right unto a man but thereof are the ways of death." (Prov. 14:14) Because there are two ways in life for your destiny, where are you heading to? There are many signs which show us the end of the world is very near. Jesus taught that when you shall hear of wars, commotions, famines, earthquakes, pestilences and fearful sights, you shall know that the end of the world is near. Many people are filled with fear by seeing the things which are coming on the earth today. But they ignore Jesus, who is the way.

There is a hidden secret in the book of God, the hour no human can tell, when scenes are to be changed on this revolving earth. Old kingdoms will fall and new kingdoms will give birth. Awake ye slumbering world, repent! You sons of men for this can only work now, for after this there will be wailing and gnashing of teeth forever.

I believe that the second coming of Jesus Christ draws near and I rejoice at this wonderful occasion. I'm prepared to meet my savior who saved me from sin. What a wonderful day this must be. But to all those who do not believe in Him, this will be a terrible day for them. It will be a day of tribulation, when God's wrath will be poured upon all unbelievers. Many people will faint with terror.

My friend, time is short. Let me ask you, do you want to attain salvation through a high standard of holiness? I expect you to say, yes. Risk it no more and receive life eternal. Surely the graces and the virtues that adorn my Christian life shines ever brighter as the end time prophecies unfold before my eyes.

Jesus said you are the light of the world. Christians, this is your world, no wonder, things are urgent and the world is on fire. I have no time to spare; I must run fast turning the fire out of full blast, while the precious wells of living water are still running out of my belly. We should take the gospel into the streets, into the highways, into the schools, and into the world. Christians, we are not laboring in vain.

My friend, the day of salvation is now, Jesus is the way. He is willing, and ready to save you now if you want—do you? He invites you to come to Him as He says, "Come unto me, all ye that labour and are heavy laden and I will give you rest." (Matt. 11:28) You will feel moving power in your heart after coming to Jesus, and that will cause you to tell others of a love that is everlasting. God bless you.

About the Author

PETER N. MUYA HAS WORKED with Full Gospel Church and Redeemed Gospel Church, before starting his own ministry, Gospel Messengers Church. He was born in 1955 in Nyonjoro farm, Lanet, Nakuru County. He has a bachelor's degree in ministry, an associate's degree in biblical studies and counseling. Other books by the author, The Gospel Messenger, Kill Me Not, Never Lose Hope, Hope For Survival, Do Not Weep and I Shall Not Die. He is married to Mary Muya, and they have three children who are adults working in different parts of our country. He is the founder and the Bishop of Gospel Messengers Church in East Africa.

ABOUT THE BOOK

"Why was I born?" peter questions his miserable life of sexual lust and drug abuse. But before he was lost forever in addiction, God's love arrested him and he took a step of faith to call Jesus Christ to deliver him from evil behaviors and he was transformed. This unconditional love that bursts in the heart went beyond the confines of his girlfriend Nelly, family and personal interests. After growing up spiritually in Kiambogo village church, the divine love exploded in his life and he went out to testify about it to his friends and neighbors. His mission is to preach the gospel to all people before it's too late. Love Without Lust gives the youth tips on how to chill out from sexual lust and drug abuse by obeying God's word and waiting until wedding day.

https://web.facebook.com/peter.n.muya

About Us

Gospel Messengers Church is a nonprofit dedicated to transforming lives in Kenya's most marginalized communities. Committed to eradicating female genital mutilation (FGM), poverty, and illiteracy, the organization builds schools, provides clean water through boreholes, and empowers communities through education and sustainable development.

By addressing social injustices and uplifting vulnerable populations, Gospel Messengers Church fosters hope and opportunity for the less fortunate.

You can Donate via M-Pesa Pay Bill no: 880100 a/c: 5146870014.

You can also use PayPal email: messengergospel13@gmail.com

THESE ARE OUR BANK DETAILS FOR INTERNATIONAL MONEY TRANSFERS.

Bank Name	NCBA BANK KENYA PLC
Branch Name	NAKURU
Branch Code	000 (for any branch)
Bank Full Address	P.O. BOX 44599–00100, NAIROBI – KENYA
Bank Account Name	GOSPEL MESSENGER CHURCH
Bank Code	07
Bank Account Number	5146870014
SWIFT /BIC Code	CBAFKENX